food by
Mark Sargeant

text by
Emily Quah

photographs by
Lisa Barber

Healthy Appetite

quadrille

notes

All spoon measures are level unless otherwise stated:
1 tsp = 5ml spoon; 1 tbsp = 15ml spoon.

All herbs are fresh, and all pepper is freshly ground black pepper unless otherwise suggested.

I recommend using free-range eggs. If you are pregnant or in a vulnerable health group, avoid those recipes that contain raw egg whites or lightly cooked eggs.

If possible, buy unwaxed citrus fruit if you are using the zest.

My timings are provided as guidelines, with a description of colour or texture where appropriate. Oven timings apply to fan-assisted ovens. If using a conventional oven, increase the temperature by 15°C (1 Gas Mark). Use an oven thermometer to check the accuracy of your oven.

contents

Introduction

Healthy eating is a topic close to my heart. I've been passionate about leading a healthy lifestyle for many years now. It started when my father-in-law signed me up for the London marathon in 2000. Back then, I was overweight and out-of-shape, but I loved the challenge and now I'm hooked. I've run every London marathon since, even a double marathon in South Africa. My personal goal is to complete ten consecutive marathons by the time I turn 45. So far, I'm on track to achieving my target.

As for maintaining a healthy lifestyle, it goes without saying that keeping fit and eating well go hand-in-hand. Any chef will tell you that we lead the most unorthodox and unhealthy lifestyles – we pick at food all day and have no time to exercise. Only on our days off are we likely to eat properly. However, I refuse to be pigeon-holed into a stereotype. With a little extra knowledge and effort, I believe anyone can make little changes that will improve their diet and everyday lifestyle.

Now, let me clarify: this is not a diet book. Those who know me know that I don't believe in faddy diets. I do, however, believe that I can prepare and serve healthy food without jeopardising taste and flavour, or drastically changing my style of cooking. Whether it's an elegant dinner party or a simple mid-week supper, a few simple adjustments are all that's needed to make our favourite meals that bit more balanced… lower in fat and calories, yet rich in energy-giving nutrients.

Choosing the right ingredients is the core of healthy eating. It's not just a matter of selecting the leanest cuts of meat and reducing the amount of fat we consume, it helps to know which ingredients are at their peak at any given time, both in terms of flavour and nutrition. Seasonality is very important to me, both at home and in the restaurants. For our latest venture in Paris, we have pledged to ensure that the vast majority of produce we use will be sourced within 100 miles of the restaurant. If a key ingredient is not available locally, then we'll simply take the dish off the menu. That's an extraordinary commitment for any restaurant!

When it comes to putting a healthy dish together, balance and moderation are key. It's not simply a matter of putting the right types of food on a plate. How the food is cooked and seasoned, and how the whole menu comes together are just as important. And I don't advocate cutting out butter and cream completely, just using a little here and there where it will really enhance the flavour of a dish. After all, a big part of living a good life is the enjoyment of food…

Healthy cooking techniques

These are my favourite ways to cook food – in order to capture and retain the flavour and nutrients, without adding excessive amounts of fat.

Steam

Steaming really locks in the nutrients. The secret is not to overcook the food, and to make sure that you season it well. Don't rush out to buy a fancy steamer if you haven't already got one. Just upturn a small flat-bottomed heatproof bowl in a large pan or wok, then put a heatproof plate on top to hold the food. Surround with boiling water and cover the pan with a lid to keep the steam in. Steaming is ideal for cooking delicate fillets of fish, lean chicken breasts and vegetables.

Poach

I love poaching fish and tender cuts of meat, such as chicken breasts and fillets of lamb or beef, as the meat remains so tender and moist. And you can enhance the flavour by poaching in a flavoured stock. Some nutrients may leak into the cooking liquor so, where possible, I'll use it in a soup, sauce or stew. Apart from fish and tender meat cuts, firm fruit is suitable for poaching – in a sugar syrup or sweetened, spiced wine.

Stir-fry

Once you've done all the chopping, stir-fries are a fast and healthy way to get supper on the table. Food needs to be cut into small similar-sized pieces that will cook quickly and evenly. Vegetables and tender cuts of meat and poultry are suitable. And, if you use a non-stick or well-seasoned wok or deep sauté pan, you'll need very little oil.

Griddle

Griddling and barbecuing are popular because they are fun ways to cook, and I love the slightly smoky quality they impart. It is best to marinate the food beforehand, as this reduces the amount of oil you'll need for cooking. A slightly acidic marinade serves the dual purpose of tenderising food and enhancing the flavour. Cuts of meat and poultry that take longer to cook, such as chicken legs, are better precooked (either by poaching or roasting), then finished off on a hot griddle pan or the barbecue.

Roast

Roasting is one of my favourite ways to cook. I always brown meat with a little olive oil at a high heat, either on the hob or in a hot oven, then roast it at a lower temperature. Browning improves the flavour of the meat and cooking it slowly thereafter keeps it tender and moist. If you like, you can use a roasting rack to allow excess fat to drip off a joint of meat. Always leave a roast to rest before carving – it makes all the difference to the succulence of the meat.

Sauté

Pan-frying or sautéeing can be unhealthy, but it all depends on the quantity of oil used. It pays to invest in a really good non-stick frying pan as this will keep the oil you'll need to a minimum. You could try using an olive oil spray, though I'm not a fan of them myself. A restrained drizzle of light olive oil is all you need. Like stir-frying, it is important to use thinly sliced, tender cuts of meat.

Braise

Braising involves browning food at high heat, then slowly cooking it with a little liquid in the pan. Generally, the pan is transferred to the oven after browning, but braising can be done on the hob if you use a tight-fitting lid. I'm very fond of pan-braising – adding just a touch of water, wine or stock to a frying pan containing browned meat, vegetables, fish or poultry, then gently simmering until cooked.

Healthy breakfast

rich in vitamin C to boost your immunity

Melon and berry salad

Serves 4

1 canteloupe melon

1 honeydew melon

300g mixed berries, such as blueberries, blackberries and raspberries

1 lime

1 orange

1–2 tsp runny honey, to drizzle

handful of mint, shredded

Halve the melons, remove and discard the seeds, then use a melon baller to carve out the flesh in balls (or simply cut it into small chunks if you prefer).

Divide the melon balls and mixed berries between individual serving bowls (or simply toss them together in a large salad bowl).

Finely grate the zests from the lime and orange over the fruit salad. Cut the lime and orange in half and squeeze a little juice over each serving. Drizzle with a little honey, then scatter over the shredded mint.

Best served slightly chilled.

Lightly spiced
dried fruit compote

high in healthy fibre, antioxidants and minerals

Serves 4

150g dried prunes

150g dried apricots

100g dried cherries or cranberries

100g dried blueberries

1 cinnamon stick

2 star anise

finely grated zest of 1 large orange

juice of 2 large oranges

100ml water

2 tbsp Grand Marnier (optional)

low-fat natural or Greek yoghurt, to serve

Put all the dried fruit in a small saucepan with the spices, orange zest and juice, water and liqueur if using. Give the mixture a stir and slowly bring to the boil. Reduce the heat to low and cover the pan with a lid.

Simmer the mixture, giving it an occasional stir, for about 8–10 minutes until the fruit is soft and plump and the liquid has reduced and is syrupy. You may need to add a splash of water towards the end if the mixture looks too dry.

Tip into a bowl and leave to cool slightly. Serve in individual bowls with natural or Greek yoghurt.

Porridge

Serves 4

150g porridge oats or medium ground oatmeal

500ml water

500ml semi-skimmed milk

pinch of fine sea salt (optional)

To serve:

4 tbsp low-fat natural or Greek yoghurt

runny honey or brown sugar

handful of toasted flaked almonds

Put the oats, water, milk and salt, if using, into a medium saucepan. Stir well, then place over a high heat until the mixture begins to boil. Turn the heat down to low and stir frequently for 5–8 minutes as the porridge bubbles and thickens. Cook until it is the consistency you like, adding a splash of water if you prefer a thinner porridge.

Take the pan from the heat and divide the porridge between warm bowls. Top each portion with a spoonful of yoghurt, a little honey or brown sugar and a scattering of toasted almonds.

Also delicious eaten with fresh fruit in season, or dried fruit compote (see left).

5 ways with oats

High in fibre, oats are hailed as a wonder food for sustaining blood sugar levels, lowering cholesterol and reducing the risk of heart disease. They are a good source of many nutrients, especially B vitamins, vitamin E, zinc, calcium, magnesium and iron.

As they are such a brilliant source of slow-release energy, oats − in the form of porridge, granola and muesli − are ideal for breakfast, because they will keep you going until lunchtime. I also like adding them to muffins, cakes and bakes, and even savoury dishes. A handful of oats mixed with fresh breadcrumbs and a little Parmesan makes a fantastic crust for baked fish or chicken, for example. Versatile and easy to use, oats are an essential in any healthy storecupboard.

1

Bircher muesli

Put 200g rolled oats in a bowl and pour on 400ml semi-skimmed milk (or enough to moisten). Cover and refrigerate for at least an hour, ideally overnight.

Coarsely grate an apple over the oats, discarding the core and pips. Stir in 1 tbsp runny honey and 150ml low-fat natural yoghurt. Add a splash of apple juice or a little more milk to loosen the mixture if it is too thick. Serve drizzled with a little more honey and topped with fresh berries and toasted walnuts. **Serves 4**

2

Granola with dried cranberries

Heat oven to 180°C/ Gas 4. In a large bowl, mix together 250g jumbo rolled oats, 50g nibbed or flaked almonds, 50g pumpkin seeds, 50g sunflower seeds, 1 tsp ground ginger and a pinch of salt. Melt 50g butter with 5–6 tbsp honey, then add the grated zest of 1 large orange. Pour over the oat mixture and stir well. Spread the mixture on a wide baking tray and bake for 15–20 minutes until golden brown, giving it a stir every 5 minutes to ensure it colours evenly. Allow to cool and crisp up, then stir in 100g dried cranberries or blueberries. Store in an airtight container until ready to eat. **Serves 4–5**

3 Banana oat muffins Heat oven to 180°C/Gas 4. Line a 12-hole muffin tin with paper cases. In a large bowl, combine 100g oats, 200g plain flour, 1½ tsp baking powder, 1 tsp bicarbonate of soda, ¼ tsp sea salt and 100g light brown sugar. Mix well and make a well in the centre. Mash 4 large ripe bananas in another bowl, with a fork. Stir in 1 beaten large egg and 60g melted butter (or light olive oil). Add to the dry mixture with 75g chopped walnuts and fold through until just combined (don't overmix). Spoon into the paper cases and bake for 20–25 minutes until brown and a skewer inserted in the middle comes out clean. **Makes 12**

4 Cranachan with blackberries Lightly toast 4 tbsp medium ground porridge oats in a dry pan, tossing frequently for 2–3 minutes until lightly golden (don't leave unattended, as it will burn easily). Tip onto a plate and leave to cool.

Whiz 200g blackberries with about 5 tbsp runny honey in a blender or food processor to a smooth purée. Tip into a large bowl and add 300ml fromage frais, 300ml reduced fat or regular crème fraîche, 1–2 tbsp whisky and all but 1 tbsp of the toasted oats. Stir the mixture a few times to create a rippled effect. Spoon into glasses and top with a few blackberries and a sprinkling of toasted oatmeal for a delectable dessert. **Serves 4**

5 Oaty walnut and cheese scones Heat oven to 180°C/Gas 4. Put 350g self-raising flour into a large bowl and stir in 2 tsp baking powder, 1 tsp fine sea salt and a pinch of cayenne pepper. Dice 60g butter and rub into the flour mix using your fingertips until it resembles fine crumbs. Stir in 150g rolled oats, 100g grated mature Cheddar and 100g chopped walnuts. Make a well in the centre and add 2 beaten large eggs and 9 tbsp buttermilk. Mix until the dough comes together, adding a little more buttermilk if needed.

Gently roll out on a lightly floured surface to a 2.5cm thickness and stamp out rounds with a 6cm cutter. Place, slightly apart, on a baking sheet, then brush the tops with milk and sprinkle with 1 tbsp rolled oats. Bake for 15–20 minutes until golden brown. Serve warm, with soft cheese and chutney. **Makes 10–12**

Buckwheat pancakes with smoked salmon

Serves 5–6

85g buckwheat flour

85g plain flour

1½ tsp baking powder

⅓ tsp fine sea salt

1 tbsp caster sugar

200ml semi-skimmed milk

1½ tsp melted butter or light olive oil

2 large egg whites

small knob of butter, for cooking

To serve:

10–12 slices of smoked salmon

6 tbsp soured cream

3–4 tbsp capers, rinsed and drained

handful of salad leaves (optional)

olive oil, to drizzle (optional)

freshly ground black pepper

Mix the flours, baking powder, salt and sugar together in a large mixing bowl. Make a well in the centre and add the milk and melted butter or oil. Gradually draw the flour mix into the centre, stirring to combine the ingredients to make a smooth batter. Leave to stand for a few minutes.

When ready to cook, whisk the egg whites in a clean bowl to firm peaks, then fold into the pancake batter. Melt a small knob of butter in each of two non-stick blini pans or one large non-stick frying pan, to lightly coat the base.

Add a small ladleful of batter to each blini pan (or two to the frying pan) and cook over a medium heat for 1½–2 minutes until golden brown on the underside. Flip the pancakes over and cook on the other side for another minute. Slide onto a warm plate and keep warm, while you cook the rest of the batter to make 10–12 pancakes in total. After the first pancake, you probably won't need to add extra butter to the pans.

Divide the pancakes between warm serving plates and drape a couple of smoked salmon slices around. Drop a spoonful of soured cream in the middle and scatter over the capers and salad leaves, if using. Drizzle with a little olive oil and grind over some black pepper.

breakfast in style

the healthier option

Full English breakfast

Serves 4

olive oil, to brush and drizzle

4 portabello mushrooms, cleaned

300g vine-ripened cherry tomatoes

sea salt and black pepper

16 rashers of smoked back bacon

8 large eggs

dash of white wine vinegar

8 slices of rye bread, toasted

Preheat the grill to the highest setting. Half-fill a wide, shallow pan with water and bring to a simmer. Line a large (or two small) baking sheet(s) with foil, then brush over with a little olive oil.

Trim the mushrooms, removing their stalks, then lay, cap side down, on the baking sheet. Place the vine tomatoes alongside. Drizzle over a little olive oil and sprinkle with a pinch each of salt and pepper. Lay the bacon rashers in a single layer on the baking sheet (the second one if using two). Place under the grill for 5 minutes until the mushrooms are tender and the bacon is golden brown around the edges.

To poach the eggs, break each one into a cup or ramekin. Add a dash of vinegar to the pan of simmering water. Whisk the water in a circular motion to create a whirlpool effect. Gently slide the eggs into the centre of the whirlpool, one at a time, then reduce the heat to a low simmer. Poach for 1½ minutes if the eggs were at room temperature, or 2 minutes if they were straight from the fridge. The whites will have set but the yolks should still be runny in the middle.

Divide the bacon, mushrooms, tomatoes and rye toasts between warm serving plates. Carefully lift out each poached egg with a slotted spoon, dab the bottom of the spoon with kitchen paper to absorb any excess water and slide onto a rye toast. Grind some pepper over the eggs and serve at once.

Herb omelette
with cherry tomatoes

Serves 1

8–10 cherry tomatoes

1 tbsp olive oil

sea salt and black pepper

3 large eggs

handful of mixed herbs, such as flat leaf parsley, chives and chervil, chopped

Halve the cherry tomatoes or cut into quarters and place in a bowl. Heat the olive oil in a non-stick omelette pan and tip in the tomatoes. Season with salt and pepper and fry over a medium heat for 1–2 minutes until the tomatoes are just soft but still retaining their shape.

Lightly beat the eggs in a bowl in the meantime. Scatter the chopped herbs over the tomatoes, then pour in the beaten eggs. Quickly stir and shake the pan to distribute the eggs and ensure they cook evenly. When they are almost set, take the pan off the heat.

Fold the omelette, using a heatproof spatula to lift one edge and tipping the pan slightly to make it easier to fold over. Slide onto a warm plate and serve immediately.

Scrambled eggs
with anchovy and asparagus

a high protein start to the day

Serves 4

250g asparagus spears

sea salt and black pepper

100g marinated anchovy fillets (available in tubs from delis and good supermarkets)

10 large free-range eggs

knob of butter

4 large basil leaves, roughly chopped

a little olive oil, to drizzle (optional)

To prepare the asparagus, snap off the woody base of the stalks. Bring a pan of salted water to the boil and blanch the asparagus spears for 3–4 minutes or until tender. Meanwhile, chop 2 anchovies very finely.

Break the eggs into a cold, heavy-based pan and add a knob of butter and the chopped anchovies. Place the pan on the lowest heat possible and, using a heatproof spatula, stir the eggs vigorously to begin with to combine the yolks with the whites, then intermittently but frequently.

As the eggs begin to set, add a little salt, some pepper and the chopped basil to the mixture. They will take about 4 minutes to scramble and you might need to keep moving the pan on and off the heat so that they don't get overheated. The scrambled eggs should still be soft and creamy.

Drain the asparagus as soon as it is ready and dab dry with kitchen paper. Divide between warm serving plates. Pile the scrambled eggs on top and drape a few anchovy fillets over each serving. If you wish, drizzle a little olive oil around the plate. Serve immediately.

Stuffed mushrooms
with ricotta and walnuts on toast

equally good on a leafy salad as a starter

Serves 4

olive oil, to drizzle

300g portabellini (baby portabello) mushrooms, cleaned

sea salt and black pepper

350g ricotta

60g (about 4 tbsp) chopped walnuts

1 oregano sprig, leaves only, chopped

2 tbsp grated Parmesan

8 slices of multi-seeded rye or sourdough bread

Heat the oven to 200°C/Gas 6. Line a large baking sheet with foil and brush over with a little olive oil. Place the mushrooms, cap side down, on the baking sheet. Sprinkle with a small pinch each of salt and pepper.

In a bowl, mix together the ricotta, walnuts, oregano, Parmesan and a little seasoning. Spread a teaspoonful of the mixture on top of each mushroom, then drizzle over a little olive oil. Bake for 10 minutes until the mushrooms are tender.

Lightly toast the bread in the meantime. Place a couple of slices on each warm serving plate and arrange the mushrooms on top. Drizzle with a little olive oil if you like and serve warm.

Berry and yoghurt smoothie

energising breakfast in a glass

Serves 4–6

200g raspberries

200g blackberries

6 heaped tbsp low-fat natural yoghurt

300ml milk

3–4 tbsp icing sugar or maple syrup, to taste

Place all the ingredients in a blender and whiz until smooth, sweetening the mixture with icing sugar or maple syrup to taste. Serve in chilled glasses.

more ideas for smoothies...

Fig, honey and yoghurt
Trim 8 ripe figs, removing the tops, then cut into quarters. Put into a blender along with 600ml semi-skimmed milk, 200ml low-fat natural yoghurt and 6–8 tbsp honey to taste. Add 4–6 ice cubes, for extra chill if you like. Blend until smooth and thick, then pour into chilled glasses. Serves 4

Pomegranate and banana
Peel 3 large ripe bananas, cut into chunks and freeze in a plastic bag for an hour. Drop the banana chunks into a blender. Scrape the seeds from a vanilla pod with the back of a knife and add them to the blender. Pour in 250ml pomegranate juice, 500ml low-fat natural yoghurt and 1–2 tbsp honey. Blend until smooth and serve in chilled glasses. Serves 4

Date, walnut and linseed bread

Makes one 900g loaf

50g unsalted butter, diced, plus extra
to grease

250g medjool dates, pitted and chopped

2 tbsp (about 30–40g) molasses

250ml water

250g plain flour

250g wholemeal flour

½ tsp fine sea salt

125g light muscovado or brown sugar

2 tsp baking powder

2 large eggs, lightly beaten

1 tsp vanilla extract

50g chopped walnuts

30g linseed

Heat the oven to 170°C/Gas 3. Butter a 900g loaf tin, preferably non-stick. Put the butter, chopped dates, molasses and water in a small pan over a low heat. Stir until the butter and molasses have melted, then take off the heat and leave to cool.

Put the flours, salt, sugar and baking powder into a large mixing bowl and stir to combine. Make a well in the centre. Add the eggs and vanilla extract, then pour the date mixture into the well. Fold through the ingredients until evenly incorporated, but don't overmix. Finally, fold through the chopped walnuts and linseed.

Spoon the mixture into the prepared tin and spread evenly. Bake for about 1 hour until a skewer inserted into the centre of the loaf comes out clean. Turn out onto a wire rack and leave to cool completely before slicing.

Delicious served just as it is, or lightly toasted with cheese.

Seeded honey loaf

enriched with nutrient-packed seeds

If using fresh yeast, put 3–4 tbsp of the water into a warm bowl, crumble in the yeast and stir to dissolve. Leave to sponge for a few minutes.

Put the flours and salt into a large mixing bowl, add the seeds and stir to mix. (If you're using fast-action dried yeast, stir this into the flour mixture.) Make a well in the centre and add the olive oil, honey, yeast mixture and remaining water (all of it if using dried yeast). Stir with a wooden spoon to combine, adding more flour if the dough seems too wet. It should be soft, but not sticky.

Press the dough into a ball, then knead on a lightly floured surface for about 5–10 minutes until smooth. Place in a lightly oiled bowl, cover with lightly oiled cling film and leave the dough to rise in a warm part of the kitchen for an hour or so until doubled in size.

Punch the dough down on a lightly floured surface and knead it lightly. Divide into two pieces and shape each one into a round loaf. Place each on a lightly oiled large baking sheet and cover with lightly oiled cling film. Leave to prove in a warm spot until almost doubled in size.

Heat the oven to 200°C/Gas 6. Remove the cling film and brush a thin layer of milk over the loaves. Bake for about 20–25 minutes until light golden in colour. The loaves should sound hollow when tapped underside. Leave to cool on a wire rack. Best served slightly warm.

Makes two 500g loaves

15g fresh yeast (or 7g sachet fast-action dried yeast)

275ml tepid water

225g wholemeal flour

225g strong white flour, plus extra to dust

1½ tsp fine sea salt

50g mixed seeds (about 2 tsp each of poppy, sesame, pumpkin, linseed and sunflower)

3 tbsp olive oil, plus extra to oil

2 tbsp honey

2 tbsp milk, to glaze

Wholemeal blueberry muffins

deliciously moist and full of goodness

Makes 12

2 very ripe large bananas

300g wholemeal flour

1½ tsp baking powder

1 tsp bicarbonate of soda

pinch of fine sea salt

100g light muscovado or brown sugar

284ml carton buttermilk

1 large egg, lightly beaten

75g light olive oil (or melted butter)

200g blueberries, rinsed and drained

1 tbsp demerara sugar

Heat the oven to 180°C/Gas 4. Line a 12-hole muffin tin with muffin cases. Peel the bananas and mash in a bowl, using a fork.

Mix the flour, baking powder, bicarbonate of soda, salt and brown sugar together in a large mixing bowl. Make a well in the centre and add the buttermilk, egg, olive oil and bananas. Quickly fold the ingredients together until just incorporated, taking care not to overmix. Tip in the blueberries and give the batter one or two stirs.

Spoon the batter into the muffin cases and sprinkle with the demerara sugar. The cases will be quite full. Bake in the oven for about 20–25 minutes until well risen and golden brown on top; a skewer inserted into the centre of the muffin should emerge clean.

Leave to cool in the tin for a couple of minutes, then transfer to a wire rack to cool completely.

getting the right balance

A varied diet that includes lots of different foods helps to ensure you are getting all the nutrients you need, but the proportion of those foods on your plate is also important. It's a matter of eating the right amount from each of the food groups: carbs; fruit and veg; protein foods; dairy foods (or equivalents); sugars and fats. It seems obvious, but not everyone has an awareness of what and how much they should be eating in a day.

Carbohydrates should provide the bulk of our food – about 50 per cent of it. These give us the energy we need and the best choices are unrefined and fibre-rich carbohydrates, such as wholegrain bread, cereals and rice, potatoes and oats.

Fruit and vegetables should comprise around a third of our food intake. These are vital sources of vitamins, minerals and fibre. The recommended amount is at least five portions a day (see pages 58–9). It's really not that difficult to achieve this.

Protein foods are vital to carnivores and vegetarians alike. We all need proteins to build and repair our bodies. These can come from fish, meat, poultry, eggs, beans, pulses, nuts and seeds. The idea is to eat a moderate amount each day, to make up around 10–15 per cent of our total intake.

Dairy products (other than butter and margarine, which are classed as fats) are an important source of calcium – vital to maintaining healthy bones – and protein. If you are lactose intolerant, goat's, sheep's and soya milk products are good alternatives. Choose reduced-fat milk and cheeses if you are controlling your calorie and fat intake.

Fats and sugars should be eaten sparingly, as we all know. Some fats are vital to health though, so it helps to understand the different types (see pages 108–9). Keep saturated and trans fats, as well as refined sugars, to a minimum.

Healthy brunch/lunch

Cod and tomato chowder

Serves 4–5

3 tbsp olive oil

2 medium onions, peeled and roughly chopped

2 celery sticks, trimmed and roughly chopped

sea salt and black pepper

2 large carrots, peeled and roughly chopped

2 large waxy potatoes, about 400g, peeled and roughly chopped

1 yellow pepper, cored, deseeded and roughly chopped

few thyme sprigs

1 bay leaf

400g tin chopped tomatoes

900ml fish or chicken stock (see pages 248–9)

150g green beans, cut into short lengths

2 courgettes, roughly chopped

few dashes of Tabasco sauce (optional)

600g cod fillets, skinned and pin-boned

bunch of flat leaf parsley, roughly chopped

Heat the olive oil in a heavy-based pan. Add the onions, celery and some seasoning, and cook, stirring, over a medium heat for 6–8 minutes to soften. Add the carrots, potatoes, yellow pepper and herbs, and sauté for 5 minutes until the vegetables are lightly golden.

Add the tomatoes to the pan and pour in the stock. Cover and simmer for about 7–9 minutes until the vegetables are tender. Now tip in the green beans and courgettes, give the mixture a stir and simmer for another 3 minutes. Check the seasoning, adding a few dashes of Tabasco to spice up the chowder if you like.

Lightly season the cod fillets and lay them on the vegetables in the pan. Cover the pan again and simmer for 3–4 minutes until the fish is opaque and just cooked through.

Using a spoon, gently break the fish into large flakes. Ladle the hot soup into warm bowls and scatter a handful of chopped parsley over each serving.

satisfying and highly nutritious

Persian-style onion soup

flavanoid-rich onions help to keep the body healthy

Serves 4

3 tbsp olive oil

5 large onions, peeled and thinly sliced

sea salt and black pepper

½ tsp ground turmeric

½ tsp fenugreek seeds

½ tsp dried mint

2 tbsp plain flour

700ml vegetable or chicken stock (see pages 248–9)

1 cinnamon stick

juice of 1 lemon

1 tsp caster sugar

few flat leaf parsley sprigs, chopped

Place a heavy-based pan over a medium heat. Add 2 tbsp olive oil, the onions and some seasoning. Cover and sweat for 12–15 minutes until the onions are soft, lifting the lid and stirring occasionally. Remove the lid and increase the heat very slightly.

Add the spices, dried mint and remaining oil, then stir in the flour. Cook, stirring frequently, for 3–4 minutes. Gradually pour in the stock, whisking as you do so to prevent any lumps forming. When it has all been added, drop in the cinnamon stick and simmer over a low heat, partially covered with the lid, for 30–40 minutes.

Stir in the lemon juice and sugar, then taste and adjust the seasoning. Discard the cinnamon stick. Ladle the soup into warm bowls and scatter over the parsley to serve.

rich in vitamin C
and healthy antioxidants

Smoked trout, orange and wild rocket salad

Serves 4

3 oranges

4 tbsp extra virgin olive oil,
to drizzle

sea salt and black pepper

200g wild rocket leaves, washed

2 hot smoked trout fillets, about
125g each

To segment the oranges, cut off the top and bottom of one and stand it upright on a board. Cut along the curve of the fruit to remove the skin and white pith, exposing the flesh. Now hold the orange over a sieve set on top of a bowl and cut out the segments, letting each one drop into the sieve as you go along. Finally, squeeze the membrane over the sieve to extract as much juice as possible. Repeat with the remaining oranges, then tip the segments into another bowl.

For the dressing, add the olive oil and a little seasoning to the orange juice that you've collected in the bowl and whisk to combine.

Add the rocket to the orange segments, then flake the smoked trout into the bowl. Add the dressing and toss gently with your hands. Pile onto individual plates and serve with pumpernickel or rye bread.

Devilled Caesar salad with Parma ham

Serves 4

8 slices of Parma ham

tiny drizzle of olive oil

8 thick slices of ciabatta

4 baby gem lettuce, trimmed and washed

15–16 (about 60g) marinated fresh anchovy fillets

Parmesan shavings, to finish

Dressing:

1 garlic clove, peeled and crushed

2 salted anchovies, rinsed, drained and finely chopped

½ tsp paprika

few dashes of Worcestershire sauce

100g natural or Greek yoghurt

freshly ground black pepper

To make the dressing, whiz all the ingredients together in a food processor, seasoning with pepper to taste. You'll probably find that the anchovies provide enough salt.

Cook the Parma ham in two batches. Heat a tiny drizzle of olive oil in a non-stick frying pan and lay half of the ham slices in the pan. Fry over a medium heat for a couple of minutes on each side until golden brown, then transfer to a plate. Cook the rest in the same way. Leave until cool and crisp, then break the Parma ham slices into smaller pieces.

Lightly toast the ciabatta slices in the same pan, turning to colour both sides. Remove and cut into chunky croûtons. Separate the lettuce leaves and divide between serving plates. Scatter over the croûtons, Parma ham and anchovies. Drizzle over the dressing and scatter over Parmesan shavings to serve.

Caesar salad with a lower fat dressing

Wild rice and basmati salad with smoked ham

perfect for a picnic lunch

Serves 4

To cook the hocks:

2 smoked ham hocks, about 800g each, soaked overnight and drained

1 onion, peeled and halved

1 large carrot, peeled and cut into 3 chunks

1 celery stick, trimmed and cut into 3 pieces

handful of flat leaf parsley sprigs

handful of thyme sprigs

1 bay leaf

½ tsp black peppercorns

Salad:

150g mixed basmati and wild rice

150g French beans, trimmed and halved

handful of flat leaf parsley, roughly torn

squeeze of lemon juice, to taste

3 tbsp extra virgin olive oil

freshly ground black pepper

Put the ham hocks into a large pan with the onion, carrot, celery, herbs and peppercorns. Pour over enough cold water to cover the hocks and bring to the boil, then skim off any scum from the surface. Cover and simmer gently for 3–4 hours until the hocks are very tender – the meat should slide easily from the bone.

Leave the hocks to cool slightly in the poaching stock, then lift onto a plate. While still warm, peel off the skin and remove the fat. Break the meat into flakes and place in a salad bowl.

Measure 1 litre of the ham poaching stock. (You can save the rest to make a soup.) Pour the measured stock into a medium saucepan and add the basmati and wild rice. Bring to the boil, lower the heat to a simmer and cook for 20–25 minutes until the rice is tender.

Blanch the green beans in the meantime. Add them to a pan of boiling salted water and cook for 3–4 minutes until just tender. Drain and refresh under cold running water. Drain thoroughly.

When ready, drain the rice in a colander set over another pan. Place the pan lid over the colander to let the rice steam and dry out a little, then tip into the bowl containing the ham. Add the beans, parsley, lemon juice, olive oil and a generous grinding of black pepper. Toss well and serve warm, or at room temperature if you prefer.

Sweet potato frittata with tomato salsa

Serves 2

1 large sweet potato, about 200–250g

1 tbsp olive oil

1 shallot, peeled and finely chopped

sea salt and black pepper

4 large eggs

small handful of chives, finely snipped

Tomato salsa:

250g vine-ripened plum tomatoes

2 spring onions, trimmed and thinly sliced on the diagonal

handful of coriander leaves, chopped

juice of ½ lemon

3 tbsp extra virgin olive oil

1 tbsp sesame oil

dash of Tabasco sauce

pinch of sugar (optional)

To make the salsa, halve or quarter the tomatoes and place in a large bowl. Add all the other ingredients and mix well, seasoning to taste with salt and pepper, and a pinch of sugar if you like. Set aside.

For the frittata, heat the grill to its highest setting. Peel the sweet potato and cut into 1cm cubes. Heat a non-stick omelette or frying pan (suitable for use under the grill) and add the olive oil. When hot, toss in the potato and shallot, and season well with salt and pepper. Cook over a medium heat, turning occasionally, for about 4–5 minutes until the potatoes are just tender and lightly golden at the edges.

Lightly beat the eggs in a bowl, add the chives and pour over the sweet potatoes. Shake the pan gently to distribute the ingredients and cook over a low heat, without stirring, for a few minutes until the eggs are beginning to set at the bottom and around the sides.

Place the pan under the hot grill briefly until the top of the frittata has set. Try not to overcook the eggs or they will turn rubbery. Leave to stand for a minute, then run a heatproof plastic spatula around the sides of the pan and invert the frittata onto a large plate. Spoon the tomato salsa into a neat pile on top and serve immediately.

Spinach and goat's cheese soufflé

Serves 8

softened butter, to grease the dishes

500g baby leaf spinach, washed

sea salt and black pepper

3 tbsp olive oil (or butter)

1 banana shallot, peeled and finely chopped

2 garlic cloves, peeled and finely crushed

40g plain flour

pinch of cayenne pepper, or to taste

250ml semi-skimmed milk

200g soft goat's cheese

2 tbsp finely grated Parmesan

4 large eggs, separated

Heat the oven to 200°C/Gas 6. Brush 8 ramekins, 150ml capacity, with very soft butter, using upward strokes. Set them on a baking tray, chill for 15 minutes, then repeat with another coating of butter.

Set a large pan over a medium-high heat. When hot, add the spinach and some seasoning. Stir for a few minutes until the leaves have wilted, adding a tiny splash of water as necessary. Tip into a colander set over a large bowl. Cool slightly, then wrap the spinach in a clean tea-towel and squeeze out the excess moisture. Chop finely and set aside.

Heat the olive oil in a medium saucepan and add the shallot and garlic. Stir over a medium heat for 4–6 minutes until soft. Add the flour and cayenne pepper and stir over a low heat for 3–4 minutes. Gradually whisk in the milk. Simmer and stir for a few more minutes until the mixture becomes thick. Transfer to a large bowl and cool slightly.

Crumble the goat's cheese into the mixture, then add the Parmesan and a little seasoning and stir to combine. Mix in the chopped spinach and egg yolks. Set aside.

Beat the egg whites in a clean bowl with an electric whisk to firm peaks, then fold into the spinach and cheese mixture until just combined. Spoon into the prepared ramekins and tap gently on the work surface to get rid of any large air pockets. Run the tip of a small knife around the edge of each one. Bake for 13–15 minutes until risen and golden brown on top. Serve immediately, with a simple side salad.

Spaghetti vongole

low in fat and a good source of minerals

Serves 4

2kg fresh palourdes (carpet shell clams) in the shell

sea salt and black pepper

300g dried spaghetti or linguine

2 tbsp olive oil

3 fat garlic cloves, peeled

1 banana shallot, peeled and roughly sliced

1 small red chilli, quartered lengthways

handful of basil stalks

75ml dry white wine

2 tbsp flat leaf parsley, finely chopped

Scrub the clams under cold running water and discard any that do not close tightly when gently tapped on the work surface. Meanwhile, bring a large pan of salted water to the boil for the pasta. When it comes to a rolling boil, add the spaghetti and cook until al dente.

Cook the clams about 6 minutes before the pasta will be ready. Heat another large pan and add the olive oil. Tip in the clams and throw in the garlic, shallot, chilli and basil stalks. Pour in the wine and cover the pan with a tight-fitting lid. Shake the pan and leave to steam for 3–4 minutes until the clams have opened. Tip the clams into a colander set over a large clean bowl. Discard any that have not opened.

Pour the clam juices back into the pan and boil for a few minutes until thickened slightly. Throw in the parsley, then taste and adjust the seasoning. Clams are naturally salty so you may find that you only need pepper.

Drain the pasta thoroughly. Immediately add to the sauce and toss to coat. Return the clams to the pan and toss again. Divide between warm plates and serve immediately, with chunks of crusty bread to mop up the juices.

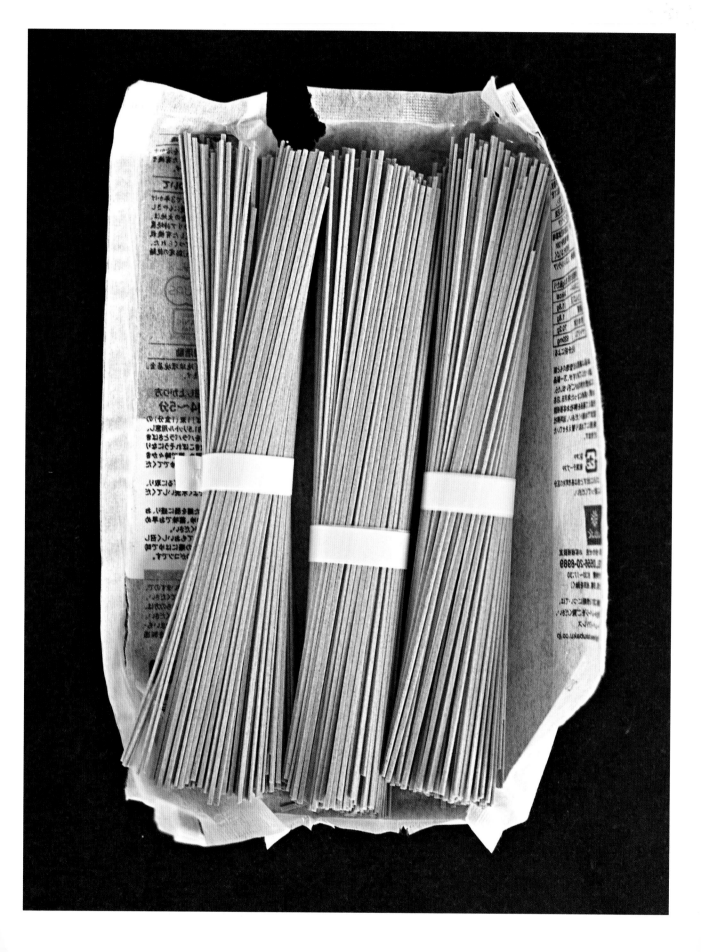

Soba noodle soup
with chicken and shiitake

light, fragrant and low in fat, yet packed with protein

Serves 4

2 large boneless, skinless chicken breasts, about 150g each

1 tbsp tamari or light soy sauce

2 tbsp mirin

1 tbsp sake

1 tbsp sesame oil, plus extra to toss

freshly ground black pepper

1.5 litres chicken stock (see page 249)

1 piece of kombu (Japanese dried kelp), lightly rinsed

3cm knob of fresh root ginger, peeled and cut into matchsticks

2–3 tbsp miso paste

200g soba noodles (Japanese buckwheat noodles)

150g shiitake mushrooms, stems trimmed and top scored

4 spring onions, trimmed and thinly sliced on the diagonal

1 tsp toasted sesame seeds, to sprinkle

First, marinate the chicken. Cut the chicken breasts across the grain into thin slices. Place in a bowl and add the tamari, mirin, sake, sesame oil and a generous grinding of pepper. Give the chicken a good stir, to ensure that every piece is coated. Cover with cling film and leave to marinate in the fridge for at least 30 minutes, or preferably overnight.

For the soup base, pour the chicken stock into a medium pan and add the kombu. Bring to a simmer, cover the pan with a lid and cook gently for 5–10 minutes. Fish out and discard the kombu, which will have imparted a lovely savoury flavour to the stock. Add the ginger and stir in the miso paste. Simmer for another 3–5 minutes.

When ready to serve, bring a pot of water to the boil for the noodles. Add the mushrooms to the simmering stock and cook for 2 minutes, then add the chicken strips. Cook until the chicken is just opaque throughout, about 1–1½ minutes. Taste and adjust the seasoning. Cover the pan with a lid and turn the heat down as low as possible.

Add the noodles to the pan of boiling water and cook until tender but still retaining a slight bite, about 3–4 minutes. Drain and immediately toss with a little sesame oil. Divide between warm soup bowls and scatter over the spring onions. Ladle the hot soup over the noodles, making sure that you divide the chicken and mushrooms evenly. Sprinkle with the sesame seeds and serve at once.

57

five-a-day

Fruit and vegetables are good sources of vitamins, minerals, antioxidants and dietary fibre – all important for boosting our immune systems and helping to prevent life-threatening illnesses such as cancer and coronary heart disease. They are also relatively low in calories, making them an ideal food for maintaining a healthy weight and lowering fat consumption.

'Five-a-day' is the recommended intake; i.e. five portions of fruit and veg in total, not five of each. This might still seem a lot, but including plenty of fruit and vegetables in your diet is easier than you think, especially as dried, preserved, tinned and frozen ones count. That said, from a nutritional angle, fresh fruit and vegetables, dried fruit and frozen foods – like peas that have been processed soon after picking – are generally the best choices.

A portion can simply be a piece of fruit, such as an apple, peach or a banana, a handful of grapes or dried apricots, a glass of fruit juice, a side salad or 100g cooked vegetables. The easiest way to meet the 'five-a-day' target is to make sure that you have at least one portion of fruit at breakfast and two portions of vegetables/fruit as part of your other meals. Raw or cooked vegetables should take up at least a third of a dinner plate. And fruit is an obvious choice for dessert, or to eat as a snack in between meals.

Vary the colour of the fruits and vegetables you eat to increase the health benefits. Different antioxidants and micro-nutrients are associated with different colours, so to get a good balance, you need to diversify your diet and aim for a colourful plate!

Healthy working lunch

Borscht

wonderfully nutritious soup that can be eaten hot or cold

Serves 4

2 tbsp olive oil

1 onion, peeled and finely chopped

2 celery sticks, trimmed and finely chopped

1 large carrot, peeled and finely chopped

1 thyme sprig, leaves stripped

sea salt and black pepper

500g raw beetroot, peeled and chopped

¼ red cabbage, about 250g, finely chopped

800ml vegetable stock (see page 248) or water

1 tbsp red wine vinegar, to taste

1 tsp caster sugar, to taste

handful of dill, chopped

4 tbsp soured cream, or natural yoghurt, to serve (optional)

Heat the olive oil in a large pan and add the onion, celery, carrot, thyme leaves and some seasoning. Cook over a medium heat, stirring frequently, for 8–10 minutes.

Add the beetroot and cabbage with a small splash of water. Stir well, then cover and cook for 10–12 minutes until the vegetables are just tender. Lift the lid and give the mixture a stir several times during cooking to stop the vegetables catching and burning on the bottom of the pan.

Remove the lid and pour in the stock or water to cover the vegetables. Add the wine vinegar, bring to the boil, then reduce the heat to a simmer. Cook for another 5–10 minutes until the vegetables are soft. Skim off any froth from the surface. Adjust the seasoning to taste with salt, pepper and sugar.

Purée the soup with a stick blender until smooth and creamy, or leave it chunky for a traditional, rustic finish. If you decide to purée the soup, you may need to thin it down slightly with a little boiling water.

Ladle into warm bowls if serving hot; otherwise allow to cool, then chill thoroughly. Serve topped with the chopped dill and a dollop of soured cream.

Chilled watercress
and spinach soup

Serves 4

2 tbsp olive oil

1 sweet onion, peeled and finely chopped

1 small potato, about 150g, peeled and diced

300g watercress, washed and thicker stalks removed

75–100g baby spinach leaves, plus a handful to garnish

800ml vegetable or chicken stock (see pages 248–9)

sea salt and black pepper

squeeze of lemon juice

3–4 tbsp crème fraîche, to serve (optional)

Heat the olive oil in a large saucepan and add the onion and potato. Sauté gently, stirring frequently, for about 10 minutes until the vegetables are soft but not brown.

Add the watercress and spinach, then pour in enough stock to cover the vegetables. Bring to the boil and season to taste with salt, pepper and a squeeze of lemon juice. As soon as the spinach and watercress have wilted, remove the pan from the heat.

Purée the soup in two batches, using a blender. Pour into a wide bowl and leave to cool completely. Cover with cling film and chill for a few hours or overnight.

To serve, pour the soup into chilled bowls and garnish with a few baby spinach leaves. Add a small dollop of crème fraîche if you wish, and grind over some pepper.

brimming with nutrients, especially vitamin C, iron and calcium

high in fibre and healthy carbs, yet low in fat

Borlotti bean minestrone

Serves 4

2 tbsp olive oil, plus a little extra to drizzle (optional)

2 onions, peeled and chopped

2 medium carrots, peeled and chopped

1 celery stick, trimmed and chopped

sea salt and black pepper

few thyme sprigs

1 bay leaf

80g smoked back bacon, trimmed of fat and chopped

2 tbsp tomato purée

2 x 400g tins borlotti beans, rinsed and drained

150g cherry tomatoes, halved

600–800ml chicken stock (see page 249) or water

75g spaghetti, broken into small pieces

large handful of basil, finely shredded

Parmesan, for grating (optional)

Heat the olive oil in a large pan and add the onions, carrots, celery and some seasoning. Stir frequently over a medium-high heat for 6–8 minutes until the vegetables are beginning to soften. Add the thyme, bay leaf and bacon. Increase the heat slightly and cook, stirring, for another 2 minutes. Stir in the tomato purée and cook for another minute.

Tip in the borlotti beans and cherry tomatoes, then pour in the chicken stock or water to cover. Bring to a gentle simmer. Add the spaghetti and cook for 10 minutes. Taste and adjust the seasoning.

To serve, ladle into warm soup bowls and scatter over the shredded basil. If you wish, add a restrained drizzle of olive oil and grate a little Parmesan over each portion. Serve with chunks of rustic country bread.

Spiced lentil soup

lentils are digested slowly, leaving you feeling full for longer

Serves 4

275g split red lentils

2 tbsp olive oil

1 large onion, peeled and finely chopped

2 large garlic cloves, peeled and finely chopped

1 tsp ground cumin

1 tsp ground coriander

2 tsp garam masala

½ tsp ground ginger

½ tsp ground turmeric

1 tbsp tomato purée

800ml vegetable or chicken stock (see pages 248–9)

To finish:

1 tbsp olive oil (optional)

1 tsp mustard seeds (optional)

1 tsp kalonji (black onion) seeds (optional)

3–4 tbsp natural yoghurt

coriander leaves

Rinse the lentils in a colander and drain well. Heat the olive oil in a medium pan and add the onion and garlic. Sauté for 4–6 minutes until lightly golden. Stir in the ground spices and tomato purée and cook for another 2 minutes.

Tip in the lentils and pour in the stock to cover. Bring to the boil, then reduce the heat. Simmer, uncovered, for 25–30 minutes or until the lentils are very soft, giving them a stir every now and then. You may need to top up with a little more water towards the end of cooking if the soup seems too thick. Taste and adjust the seasoning.

Ladle half of the soup into a blender and whiz to a purée, then pour back into the pan. The soup should be somewhat chunky. Adjust the consistency again if necessary, adding a little boiling water to thin it down.

For a little extra spice and fragrance if required, heat the 1 tbsp olive oil in a small pan and tip in the mustard and black onion seeds. When they begin to pop, pour the mixture over the soup and stir.

Ladle the soup into warm bowls and top with a spoonful of yoghurt and a few coriander leaves. Serve with warm Indian bread on the side.

Tabbouleh with goat's cheese

a range of vital nutrients and lots of fibre

Serves 4

150g bulgar wheat

sea salt and black pepper

4 spring onions

3 ripe plum tomatoes

bunch of flat leaf parsley, chopped

bunch of mint, chopped

finely grated zest of 1 lemon

2 tbsp lemon juice

2 tbsp extra virgin olive oil, plus extra to drizzle (optional)

pinch of caster sugar (optional)

150g soft goat's cheese

Put the bulgar wheat into a saucepan and pour on enough water to cover by 3–4cm. Add some seasoning and bring to the boil, then reduce the heat slightly. Simmer for about 12–15 minutes until the bulgar wheat is tender but still retains a bite.

In the meantime, trim and finely slice the spring onions on the diagonal. Halve, deseed and finely chop the tomatoes and place in a salad bowl with the spring onions. Trim the herb bunches, discarding the thicker stalks, then chop them fairly finely and add to the bowl.

When it is ready, drain the bulgar wheat in a colander or sieve and leave to dry out for a few minutes. Tip into the salad bowl, then add the lemon zest and juice, olive oil, sugar if required, and seasoning to taste. Toss to mix. Crumble over the goat's cheese, and drizzle over a little olive oil if you wish.

Note If you're preparing this salad for a packed lunch, leave the bulgar wheat to cool completely before tossing with the herbs, tomatoes and onions.

Rice noodle salad
with prawns and Thai dressing

Serves 2–3

100g thin rice noodles

drizzle of sesame oil

200g mangetout or sugar snap peas

1 large red pepper

1 large yellow or orange pepper

2 spring onions

200g peeled, cooked prawns

handful of coriander leaves

1 tbsp toasted black or white sesame seeds, to sprinkle

Dressing:

1 shallot, peeled and finely diced

2 garlic cloves, peeled and finely crushed

1 small red chilli, deseeded and finely chopped

2–3 tbsp lime juice, or more to taste

2 tbsp fish sauce

1 tbsp light soy sauce

2½ tbsp palm sugar (or soft brown sugar)

2 tbsp toasted sesame oil

Bring the kettle to the boil. Place the rice noodles in a large heatproof bowl and pour on boiling water, ensuring that the noodles are fully immersed. Cover the bowl with cling film and leave to stand for 5 minutes or until the noodles are tender but still retaining a bite. Drain and immediately toss with a drizzle of sesame oil to stop them sticking to each other.

In the meantime, blanch the mangetout in a pan of boiling water for 2 minutes until they are just tender but still bright green. Refresh in a bowl of iced water, then drain well. Cut the mangetout on the diagonal into 2 or 3 pieces. Halve, core and deseed the peppers, then cut into long, thin slices. Trim and finely slice the spring onions on the diagonal.

For the dressing, put all the ingredients into a bowl and whisk lightly to combine.

Put the prawns, spring onions, mangetout and peppers into a large bowl and add the drained noodles, coriander leaves and sesame seeds. Pour the dressing over the salad and toss well to coat. Eat immediately or chill until ready to serve.

Note If you're preparing this salad for a packed lunch, leave the noodles to cool completely before tossing with the other ingredients.

Flatbread, feta and chickpea salad

tasty, nutritious and sustaining

Serves 3–4

2 large, thin flatbreads or pita breads

½ tsp paprika

4 tbsp olive oil

1 red onion, peeled and thinly sliced

2 garlic cloves, peeled and thinly sliced

½ red chilli, deseeded and finely chopped

400g tin chickpeas, rinsed and drained

generous squeeze of lemon juice

large handful of flat leaf parsley leaves

sea salt and black pepper

150g feta cheese

Heat the oven to 180°C/Gas 4. Split the breads horizontally. Mix the paprika with 2 tbsp of the olive oil. Brush each piece of bread with this mixture and place on a baking sheet. Bake until lightly golden brown and crisp, just 2–3 minutes for thin flatbreads, 4–5 minutes for pita bread.

Meanwhile, heat the remaining olive oil in a pan, add the onion and cook, stirring, over a medium heat for 6–8 minutes until soft. Add the garlic and chilli and fry for another minute. Tip in the chickpeas and stir to mix. Squeeze over the lemon juice and add the parsley and a little seasoning to taste.

Warm the chickpeas through, then tip into a large bowl and leave to stand for a few minutes. Crumble over two-thirds of the cheese and toss well. Divide between serving plates and crumble over the remaining feta. Break the bread into smaller pieces and serve on the side.

Note If you're preparing this salad for a packed lunch, leave the chickpea mixture to cool completely before adding the feta. Pack the bread in a separate airtight container to keep it crisp.

Creole spiced bean
and vegetable salad

high in fibre, low in fat and plenty of slow-release energy

Serves 6

2 tbsp olive oil

1 onion, peeled and thinly sliced

sea salt and black pepper

200g French beans, trimmed

2 courgettes, trimmed and sliced into
1½cm rounds

8 spring onions, trimmed and cut into
short lengths

400g tin haricot or butter beans, rinsed
and drained

400g tin cannellini beans, rinsed and
drained

400g tin chickpeas, rinsed and drained

250g cherry tomatoes, halved

bunch of flat leaf parsley, leaves only,
roughly chopped

bunch of coriander, leaves only,
roughly chopped

Creole spice mix:

1½ tsp sweet paprika

1½ tsp dried basil

1½ tsp dried thyme

pinch of cayenne pepper, or to taste

pinch of chilli powder, or to taste

Heat the olive oil in a pan and add the onion with some salt and pepper. Stir frequently over a medium heat for 6–8 minutes until the onion is soft.

Meanwhile, combine the ingredients for the Creole spice mix in a small bowl. Add to the pan and stir for another minute or two until fragrant.

Tip the French beans, courgettes and spring onions into the pan and cook for 6–8 minutes until tender. Turn off the heat, add the tinned beans and chickpeas along with the cherry tomatoes, and toss to mix.

Transfer the salad to a large bowl and stir in the chopped parsley and coriander. Serve slightly warm or at room temperature.

5 ways with oily fish

Sardines, mackerel, tuna and other oily fish are rich in omega-3 fatty acids. These essential nutrients offer a range of benefits – not least for a healthy brain, eyes and skin. Growing up, I used to cringe at the thought of swallowing a spoonful of cod liver oil… little did I know then that oily fish are a much better source of omega-3's. The fish must, however, be fresh – tinned tuna, sardines etc., won't give you the same benefits because most of those omega-3's are lost in the canning process. Not only are oily fish like mackerel, pilchards and sardines healthy, they are also abundant – and some of the cheapest fish available. As a nation we really should be eating more of them...

1 Escabeche of mackerel
Season 4 filleted, pin-boned mackerel and lay in a lightly oiled wide dish. Heat 2–3 tbsp olive oil in a saucepan and add 1 finely sliced large carrot, 1 finely sliced banana shallot, 2 star anise, a pinch of saffron strands, ½ tsp crushed coriander seeds and a pinch of salt. Fry for 2–3 minutes, then add 50ml white wine vinegar, 150ml dry white wine and 1 tbsp caster sugar. Simmer for 5 minutes, then adjust the seasoning. Pour the hot marinade over the fish and cool. Cover with cling film and chill overnight. Serve at room temperature, scattered with chopped coriander leaves, with crusty bread on the side. The mackerel is best eaten without the skin. **Serves 4**

2 Smoked mackerel and fennel salad
Shave 2 large fennel bulbs, using a mandolin. Immerse in iced water for 10 minutes to crisp up. Drain well and tip into a salad bowl. Flake 2 peppered smoked mackerel fillets (about 160g) and add to the fennel. For the dressing, whisk together 1½ tbsp grainy mustard, 1½ tbsp runny honey, 1½ tbsp lemon juice, 6–7 tbsp extra virgin olive oil and some seasoning. Add a handful of chopped dill to the fennel with the dressing and toss well. **Serves 4**

3 **Herrings with mustard and dill** For the sauce, peel and deseed 1 small cucumber, then grate and squeeze out the excess water. Mix with a handful of chopped dill, 200g natural yoghurt, the juice of ½ lemon, salt, pepper and a pinch of paprika.

Fillet 4 cleaned whole herrings (about 250g each) and check for pin-bones, then brush 2 tbsp mustard over the boned sides. Mix 4–5 tbsp porridge oats with 1 tsp thyme leaves and use to coat the herring fillets. Heat 1–2 tbsp olive oil in a non-stick frying pan and fry the fish for about a minute on each side. Serve immediately, with the sauce. **Serves 4**

4 **Seared tuna with Swiss chard** Season 4 tuna steaks, each 150g and 2cm thick. Sprinkle with chopped coriander, drizzle over a little olive oil and leave to marinate for 10 minutes. Separate the leaves and stalks of a large bunch of Swiss chard. Thinly slice the stalks and roughly chop the leaves. Heat a little olive oil in a large pan and lightly fry 2 finely chopped garlic cloves and 1 finely chopped deseeded red chilli. Add the chard stalks, some seasoning and a little splash of water. Cover and cook for 5 minutes. Tip in the leaves and cook for another 3–5 minutes until tender. Season the tuna steaks and sear in a non-stick frying pan for 1–1½ minutes each side. Rest for a few minutes, then serve with the chard. **Serves 4**

5 **Tomato and olive crusted trout fillets** Heat oven to 200°C/Gas 6. Lightly season 4 skinless trout fillets, about 130g each, and place on a lightly oiled baking tray, skinned side up. For the crust, in a bowl, mix 100g fresh breadcrumbs with 1 crushed garlic clove, 30g chopped sun-dried tomatoes, 30g chopped pitted black olives and 1–2 tbsp olive oil. Roughly chop a handful of basil leaves and add to the bowl. Toss to mix and season to taste. Spread the crust over each trout fillet, patting down lightly with the back of the spoon. Bake for 10–12 minutes until the crust is golden and and crisp. Serve at once, with minted new potatoes if you like. **Serves 4**

Glazed salmon
with spinach and radish salad

Serves 4

4 lightly smoked salmon fillets, 125–150g each

100g baby spinach leaves, washed and dried

8–10 radishes, washed, trimmed and finely sliced

Marinade:

3 tbsp honey

1 tbsp lemon juice

2 tbsp light soy sauce

1 tsp Dijon mustard

½ tsp grated fresh root ginger

Dressing:

1 tbsp grated fresh root ginger

3 tbsp rice wine vinegar

2 tbsp light soy sauce

2 tbsp sesame oil

2–3 tbsp tahini

Remove the skin from the salmon and check carefully for pin-bones, pulling out any with kitchen tweezers. Place the fillets side by side in a shallow dish. For the marinade, mix the ingredients together in a bowl, then pour over the salmon to coat. Cover with cling film and leave to marinate in the fridge for 30 minutes to allow the flavours to permeate.

For the dressing, whisk together all the ingredients in a bowl and set aside.

Heat the oven to 230°C/Gas 8. Arrange the spinach leaves on individual plates and top with the radish slices.

Lift the salmon from the marinade and arrange on a lightly oiled baking tray. Cook in the oven for 4–6 minutes until medium rare, basting after 2 minutes. The fish should feel slightly springy when pressed.

Place a salmon fillet in the middle of each plate and drizzle the ginger and tahini dressing over the salad to serve.

Note If you're preparing this salad for a packed lunch, allow the salmon to cool and pack the dressing and salad leaves in separate containers. Assemble just before eating.

packed with essential nutrients

Mango, avocado and smoked chicken salad

Serves 4

2 medium, firm but ripe mangoes

2 ripe avocados

squeeze of lemon juice

300–350g smoked chicken breasts

200g mixed salad leaves, such as rocket, mâche, baby chard or amaranth

2 tbsp pine nuts, toasted (optional)

Dressing:

2 tbsp orange juice

2 tbsp lemon juice

1 tbsp wholegrain mustard

2 tbsp extra virgin olive oil

2 tbsp avocado oil (or olive oil)

sea salt and black pepper

Peel the mangoes and cut the flesh away from the stone into thin slices. Arrange on four serving plates.

Halve the avocados and remove the stone. Peel off the skin and slice the flesh into strips. Squeeze over a little lemon juice to stop the flesh discolouring, then arrange over the mango slices.

Cut the chicken into thin slices and divide between the plates. Neatly pile the salad leaves in the middle.

For the dressing, whisk the ingredients together in a bowl, seasoning with salt and pepper to taste. Spoon the dressing over the salad and serve, topped with a handful of toasted pine nuts if you like.

Note If you're preparing this salad for a packed lunch, pack the dressing and salad in separate containers and combine just before eating.

healthy snacks

Snacking gives you an energy boost, which you may need – even between healthy meals – if you're very active. It's what you eat that makes a difference. So, ditch the bag of crisps and make healthy choices to curb hunger pangs:

Dried fruits and nuts These are concentrated sources of many nutrients. Dried apricots, for example, are high in fibre, vitamins and minerals. Nuts are a good source of protein and minerals; walnuts, in particular, are rich in essential fats.

Healthy dips Swap fattening crisps for vegetable sticks and serve with homemade dips so that you can control the amount of oil added. Avocados are great for making guacamole and they're rich in good fats, vitamins and minerals.

Low-fat yoghurts Choose from cow's, sheep or goat's milk yoghurts, which are loaded with calcium but without the excess fat and calories. Eat with a drizzle of natural honey or some dried fruit compote.

Oats Whether they come in the form of oatcakes, muffins, scones or cereal bars, oats are the perfect food for snacking on, because they release energy slowly as the body takes time to digest them. Just be mindful of the high amount of sugar and fat in most commercially produced cereal bars and bakes.

Smoothies Make your own using bananas, reduced-fat yoghurt and virtually any tangy fruit you fancy. Smoothies keep you feeling full for longer, too.

Chocolate Yes, eating too much will make your thighs bigger but a little good quality dark chocolate is a useful source of antioxidants. A few squares (not the whole bar) will suffice.

Fresh fruit 'An apple a day keeps the doctor away...'

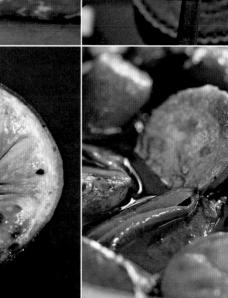

Healthy Sunday lunch

Baked sea bass
with lemon couscous

healthy white fish – low in fat, high
in protein and B vitamins

Serves 4

1 sea bass, about 1.1kg, scaled and gutted

sea salt and black pepper

olive oil, to drizzle

few rosemary sprigs

handful of large basil leaves

2 large garlic cloves, peeled and thinly sliced

½ lemon, cut into wedges

Couscous:

250g couscous

finely grated zest of 1 lemon

1 tender rosemary sprig, leaves stripped and finely chopped

300ml boiling water or chicken stock (see page 249)

250g peas, thawed if frozen

juice of ½ lemon

4 tbsp extra virgin olive oil

bunch of flat leaf parsley, chopped

Heat the oven to 200°C/Gas 6. Score the sea bass on both sides and rub all over with salt, pepper and a little drizzle of olive oil. Pick the rosemary sprigs off the hard stems. Roll a large basil leaf tightly around each rosemary sprig. Insert into the slashes in the fish, along with the garlic slices.

Lay the sea bass on a lightly oiled foil-lined baking tray. Stuff the cavity with the lemon wedges and remaining rosemary. Bake for 15–20 minutes until the flesh is opaque and just cooked through – you should be able to pull out a fin easily.

Prepare the couscous while the fish is in the oven. Put the couscous, lemon zest, chopped rosemary and some seasoning into a large bowl and pour over the boiling water or stock. Cover with cling film and leave for 5 minutes. Meanwhile, cook the peas in boiling water for 3–4 minutes until tender.

For the dressing, mix the lemon juice with the olive oil and some seasoning to taste. Once the couscous has absorbed all the liquid, fluff it up with a fork. Drain the peas and add to the couscous along with the dressing and chopped parsley. Toss to mix.

Serve the fish with the warm couscous and steamed pak choi or green beans.

Note To serve eight, cook two sea bass of this size rather than a larger fish and make double the quantity of couscous.

Marinated halibut
with spiced aubergines

Serves 4

6 skinless halibut fillets, about 130g each

3 tbsp olive oil

sea salt and black pepper

¾ tsp ground turmeric

Spiced aubergines:

3 large aubergines

5 tbsp olive oil

3 large onions, peeled and finely sliced

2 tsp ground cumin

3 plum tomatoes, skinned, deseeded and chopped

150g sultanas, soaked in hot water for 10 minutes

2–3 tbsp lemon juice, to taste

handful of basil leaves, torn

Lay the fish in a shallow dish and drizzle over the olive oil. Sprinkle with pepper and the turmeric, and rub all over to coat evenly. Cover with cling film and leave to marinate in the fridge for a few hours, or for at least 20 minutes.

Heat the oven to 200°C/Gas 6. Cut the aubergines into 3cm chunks, sprinkle with salt and leave to stand in a colander set over a bowl for 20 minutes. (Doing this prevents them from absorbing as much oil during cooking.)

Rinse the aubergines to remove the salt, drain well and pat dry with kitchen paper. Toss them in a large baking tray with some black pepper and about 2–3 tbsp olive oil. Bake for about 20–25 minutes until the aubergines are soft.

Meanwhile, heat the remaining 2 tbsp olive oil in a pan. Add the onions with some seasoning and sweat over a medium heat for 8–10 minutes until soft. Add the cumin and fry for a few more minutes until the onions are lightly caramelised. Take off the heat. When the aubergines are ready, add them to the onions with the tomatoes, sultanas, lemon juice and salt and pepper to taste.

To cook the fish, heat a large non-stick frying pan and fry the fish fillets for 2 minutes on each side – they should feel just firm when lightly pressed. Leave to rest for a minute or two, while you reheat the spiced aubergines. Pile these onto warm plates and top with the halibut fillets. Scatter the basil around and drizzle over a little turmeric oil from the pan.

91

Roast chicken
with baby vegetables

buy organic or free-range chicken for the best flavour

Serves 4–6

1 large chicken, about 1.8–2kg

sea salt and black pepper

1 tbsp olive oil, plus a little extra
to drizzle

1 head of garlic, halved horizontally

2 lemons, halved

handful of thyme sprigs

few rosemary sprigs

300g baby carrots, scrubbed

300g baby turnips, washed and halved
if quite large

100ml dry white wine

300ml chicken stock (see page 249)

Heat the oven to 230°C/Gas 8. Rub the chicken all over with salt, pepper and a little drizzle of olive oil. Place in a large roasting pan and stuff the cavity with half the head of garlic, 2 or 3 lemon halves and a few herb sprigs.

Roast the chicken for 20 minutes, then take it out of the oven and lower the setting to 200°C/Gas 6. Add the carrots and turnips to the roasting pan and turn to baste in the juices. Put the remaining garlic, lemon halves and herbs around the chicken. Drizzle a little olive oil over the bird and vegetables, and sprinkle with a little salt and pepper. Roast for another 35–40 minutes or until the bird is golden brown and cooked through – the juices should run clear when the thickest part of the thigh is pierced with a knife.

When ready, lift the chicken onto a warm platter, cover with foil and leave to rest for 10–15 minutes in a warm place. Put the vegetables into a warm dish, cover and keep hot.

Meanwhile, skim off any fat from the cooking juices in the roasting pan, then place on the hob over a medium heat. Add the wine, scraping up the sediment from the bottom of the tray to deglaze and let bubble until reduced by half. Pour in the stock and again boil until reduced by half. Add any juices from the rested chicken, then strain into a warm jug.

Carve the chicken and divide the meat and roasted vegetables between warm plates. Pour the sauce over the chicken. Serve with new potatoes and a green vegetable, such as broccoli or Brussels sprouts.

Serves 5

olive oil, to drizzle

10 chicken drumsticks

sea salt and black pepper

Glaze:

6 tbsp honey

3 tbsp fish sauce

1½ tbsp light soy sauce

juice of 1½ lemons

3 tbsp rice wine vinegar

1½ tbsp sesame oil

Heat the oven to 200°C/Gas 6. Lightly oil a large baking dish. Season the drumsticks with salt and pepper and arrange in the dish in a single layer. Drizzle over a little olive oil and bake in the hot oven for 20 minutes.

Prepare the glaze in the meantime. Mix all the ingredients together in a small bowl until evenly combined.

Take the chicken out of the oven and pour over the glaze, to coat each drumstick. Return to the oven and bake for another 20–30 minutes, turning several times, until the chicken is tender and nicely glazed.

Let the chicken rest for a few minutes before serving. For a balanced meal, serve with steamed rice and purple sprouting broccoli or green beans.

Pheasant and ginger casserole

Serves 4

2 oven-ready pheasants, about 750g each

sea salt and black pepper

2 large carrots, peeled and each cut into 3 chunks

2 large celery sticks, trimmed and each cut into 3 pieces

200g cipollini or baby onions, peeled

2 x 5cm knobs of fresh root ginger, halved lengthways

1 head of garlic, halved horizontally

handful of thyme sprigs

few rosemary sprigs

5 cloves

2 star anise (optional)

1 tsp black peppercorns

Rub the pheasants all over with a little salt and pepper and lay them breast side down in a large cast-iron pan or other flameproof casserole. Add the carrots, celery and onions, along with the ginger, garlic, herbs, cloves, star anise if using, and peppercorns. Pour in enough water to come two-thirds of the way up the sides of the pheasants.

Place over a high heat and bring to the boil. Immediately lower the heat to a simmer, partially cover the pan with a lid and cook gently for 35–40 minutes until the pheasants are tender, turning them over halfway through cooking.

To serve, lift the pheasants out of the broth and either carve them into smaller joints or remove the meat from the carcass and break into shreds. Divide between warm bowls and ladle over the hot broth and vegetables. Serve with chunks of rustic bread.

Roasted fillet of beef with tomato tarragon dressing

red meat is an excellent source of protein and iron

Serves 6

1.2kg prime beef fillet (in one piece, cut from the thick end)

sea salt and black pepper

2 tbsp olive oil

few handfuls of wild rocket leaves

Tomato tarragon dressing:

500g (about 6) ripe plum tomatoes

5 tbsp homemade ketchup (see page 125)

2 tbsp Worcestershire sauce

1 tbsp Dijon mustard

few dashes of Tabasco sauce

juice of 1 lemon

2 tbsp balsamic vinegar

2 tbsp extra virgin olive oil

2 shallots, peeled and finely chopped

large handful each of tarragon and flat leaf parsley, chopped

To make the dressing, cut each tomato in half and squeeze out the seeds. Finely chop the flesh and place in a large bowl. Add the rest of the ingredients except for the herbs, and mix well. Season well with salt and pepper to taste. Cover with cling film and chill for at least 20 minutes or until ready to serve.

Heat the oven to 200°C/Gas 6 and preheat a roasting pan. Trim any fat or sinew from the fillet of beef and season all over with salt and pepper. Heat a non-stick frying pan with a little olive oil. When it is very hot, add the beef and sear for 1½–2 minutes on each side until evenly browned all over. Lightly oil the hot roasting pan.

Transfer the beef to the roasting pan and place in the oven. Roast for 25 minutes for medium rare beef – it should feel a little springy when lightly pressed. Transfer the fillet to a warm platter and leave to rest for 10 minutes.

Serve the beef warm or at room temperature. Slice it thickly and overlap the slices on a serving platter. Pile the rocket into the centre. Stir the chopped herbs into the tomato tarragon dressing and spoon over the beef. Accompany with new potatoes if you like.

Spicy beef curry

Serves 8–10

2kg good quality lean braising beef or chuck steak

sea salt and black pepper

4 tsp garam masala

4 tbsp natural yoghurt

4–5 tbsp light olive oil

4 large sweet onions, peeled and finely chopped

4 garlic cloves, peeled and finely chopped

5cm knob of fresh root ginger, peeled and finely grated

4 tbsp tomato purée

2 tbsp caster sugar, or to taste

2 x 400g tins chopped tomatoes

800ml beef stock (see page 249)

small handful of coriander, leaves separated, stalks finely chopped

6–8 cardamom pods

15–20 curry leaves

6 long green chillies

Spice mix:

4 tsp coriander seeds

4 tsp cumin seeds

1 tsp fennel seeds

1 tsp fenugreek seeds (optional)

4 tsp mild curry powder

1 tsp ground turmeric

Cut the beef into bite-sized chunks, put into a bowl and season with salt and pepper. Sprinkle with the garam masala, add the yoghurt and toss to coat. Cover with cling film and leave to marinate in the fridge for at least 30 minutes, or overnight. Remove and set aside before you start to prepare the curry.

For the spice mix, toast the coriander, cumin, fennel, and fenugreek if using, in a dry pan, tossing over a high heat for a few minutes until the seeds are fragrant. Tip into a mortar, add a pinch of salt and grind to a fine powder. Stir in the curry powder and turmeric.

Heat a thin film of olive oil in a large cast-iron casserole or a heavy-based pan. Add the onions, garlic, ginger and a little salt and pepper. Stir, then cover and cook for 8–10 minutes until the onions are soft, lifting the lid to give the mixture a stir a few times.

Add a little more oil, tip in the ground spice mix and cook, stirring, for 2 minutes. Add the tomato purée and sugar and stir over a medium-high heat for a few minutes until the onions are lightly caramelised. Add the tomatoes, beef stock, coriander stalks, cardamom pods, curry leaves and whole green chillies.

Add the beef and stir until well coated in the sauce, then partially cover the pan with a lid. Simmer very gently, stirring occasionally for 3–4 hours, depending on the cut of beef, until the meat is meltingly tender.

To serve, ladle the curry into warm bowls and scatter over the coriander leaves. Accompany with a steaming bowl of basmati rice or warmed Indian bread.

Venison pie with sweet potato topping

Serves 4–5

600g haunch of venison

sea salt and black pepper

3 tbsp plain flour

3–4 tbsp olive oil

2 leeks, white part only, sliced thickly

150g baby onions, peeled

250g small Chantenay carrots, scrubbed

250g chestnuts mushrooms, halved

1 large rosemary sprig, leaves only

150ml red wine or port

650ml chicken stock (see page 249)

150g new potatoes, scrubbed

Sweet potato topping:

500g sweet potatoes

350g Desirée potatoes

20g butter

50g double Gloucester cheese, grated

2 large egg yolks

Cut the venison into 2.5–3cm chunks. Season the flour and use to coat the venison. Heat 2 tbsp olive oil in a large flameproof casserole and fry the meat in batches until evenly browned, about 2 minutes each side. Transfer to a bowl; set aside.

Add the leeks, onions and carrots to the casserole with a little more oil and stir over a medium heat for 4–5 minutes until lightly coloured. Add the mushrooms and rosemary and cook for a minute. Pour in the wine, scraping the bottom of the pan with a wooden spoon to deglaze. Bubble until reduced right down.

Pour in the stock and bring to a simmer. Return the venison, with any juices released, to the pan. Partially cover with a lid and gently braise for 40–50 minutes until the venison is tender, giving the mixture a stir every once in a while.

About 15 minutes before the venison will be ready, slice the new potatoes into 1cm thick rounds. Season and fry in a little olive oil in a wide non-stick frying pan until golden brown on both sides. Add to the casserole to finish cooking. Once the potatoes and venison are tender, remove the pan from the heat and let cool slightly.

For the topping, peel all the potatoes and cut into 5cm chunks. Cook in a pan of salted water for 15 minutes or until tender. Drain well and mash with a potato ricer back into the pan. While still hot, add the butter, cheese and some seasoning. Mix well to combine. Cool slightly, then mix in the egg yolks.

Heat the oven to 220°C/Gas 7. Tip the venison mixture into a large pie dish or a shallow cast-iron pan and top with the mash. Rough up the surface with a fork. Bake for 20 minutes until the topping is golden brown and the filling is bubbling around the sides. Grind over some pepper and serve.

buy prime quality
meat for optimum flavour

Roast lamb
with paprika and oranges

Serves 6–8

1 part-boned leg of lamb, about 2.4kg, with knuckle bone left in

1 tsp sweet paprika

1 tsp smoked paprika

1 tsp ground ginger

sea salt and black pepper

little drizzle of olive oil

4–5 garlic cloves, halved with skins left on

2 oranges, sliced

Heat the oven to 220°C/Gas 7. Trim away any excess fat from the lamb, then lightly score the surface fat in a criss-cross pattern. Mix the sweet and smoked paprika with the ground ginger and a pinch each of salt and pepper. Rub all over the lamb, including the boned-out cavity, with a little olive oil. Place the lamb on a rack over a large roasting pan and stuff the boned cavity with the garlic cloves and half of the orange slices. Pour a splash of water into the pan.

Roast the lamb in the hot oven for 20 minutes, then reduce the oven setting to 190°C/Gas 5 and roast for a further 20 minutes per 500g for pink lamb. If during roasting the top appears to be darkening too quickly, cover with foil. About 30 minutes before you calculate the lamb will be ready, lay the remaining orange slices over the meat.

Transfer the lamb to a warm platter, cover loosely with foil and leave to rest in a warm place for 10 minutes before carving.

When ready to serve, carve the lamb into thin slices and serve with new potatoes and a leafy salad.

Glazed gammon
with pineapple salsa

Serves 6

1 unsmoked boned gammon joint, about 2.6kg, soaked overnight

1 large carrot, peeled and cut into 3 chunks

1 large onion, peeled and halved

2 large celery sticks, cut into 3 chunks

1 bay leaf

few thyme sprigs

1 tsp black peppercorns

about 30–40 cloves

a little oil, for oiling

3 tbsp marmalade

3cm knob of fresh root ginger, peeled and finely grated

2 tbsp light soy sauce

2–3 tbsp water

Pineapple salsa:

1 large ripe pineapple

1 small cucumber

1 red chilli, finely chopped

handful of coriander, leaves only, chopped

handful of mint, leaves only, chopped

sea salt and black pepper

1 tbsp sesame oil

2 tbsp olive oil

few dashes of Tabasco sauce

juice of ½ lemon

Drain the gammon and place in a large cooking pot. Cover with fresh water, bring to the boil and allow to bubble gently for 5–10 minutes. Skim off the scum and froth that rise to the surface, then pour off the water and re-cover the joint with fresh cold water. Bring to the boil, skim, then turn the heat down to a simmer and add the vegetables, herbs and peppercorns. Simmer for about 2 hours, checking the liquid from time to time and topping up with hot water as necessary.

Lift the gammon out of the pot onto a chopping board and leave to cool slightly. (If the liquor is not too salty, save it to make a pea and ham soup.) While still warm, cut away and discard the skin and most of the fat, leaving an even layer. Score lightly in a criss-cross pattern, then stud a clove in the middle of each scored diamond.

Heat the oven to 190°C/Gas 5. Place the gammon in a lightly oiled roasting pan. Mix together the marmalade, ginger, soy sauce and water to make a glaze and brush all over the gammon to coat evenly. Roast for 20–25 minutes, basting several times, until browned and nicely glazed. You may need to turn the pan around halfway through to ensure that the joint colours evenly.

Make the salsa in the meantime. Cut away the peel and 'eyes' from the pineapple, then slice and remove the core. Cut the slices into 1cm cubes and place in a large bowl. Peel the cucumber, halve lengthways and scoop out the seeds, then finely dice the flesh. Add to the pineapple with all the other ingredients and mix well. Let stand for at least 20 minutes.

Rest the cooked gammon, covered with foil, in a warm place for 15 minutes. Carve into thin slices and serve with the pineapple salsa and vegetables of your choice.

Avoid the bad fats

A fat-free diet isn't something I'd advocate, not only because I cannot cook without olive oil and a little butter, but because it is actually healthy to consume a small amount of fat. The idea is to eat much less of the bad stuff and a bit more of the good stuff. It certainly helps to understand what's what.

Olive oil is considered to be one of the better fats to use in cooking. Like rapeseed, groundnut and avocado oils, it is classed as monounsaturated fat, which is effective in lowering bad cholesterol and raising good cholesterol.

Other vegetable oils, such as sunflower, corn, soy, walnut and safflower oils, are classed as polyunsaturated oils. These are also deemed to be heart healthy if consumed in moderation. They also provide essential fatty acids, those all-important omega-3's and omega-6's, and can lower bad cholesterol.

Saturated fats are mostly found in animal products, such as red meat, butter, lard, hard cheeses, creams and whole milk, as well as palm oil. They increase both good and bad cholesterol and should be eaten in moderation. To cut down on these fats, choose lean cuts of meat and trim off most of the fat before cooking. Use butter and cream sparingly in cooking and don't, as a matter of course, spread butter on bread – a good quality rustic loaf tastes just as good without it.

Hydrogenated oils used in processed foods, commercially baked pastries, shortenings and certain margarines are referred to as trans fats or trans fatty acids. These fats have a devastating effect on good health because they increase bad cholesterol and lower good cholesterol. Needless to say, it's best to consume as little of these as possible.

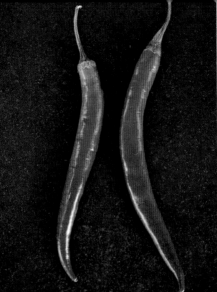

Healthy barbecues

Squid with roasted peppers and cannellini beans

Serves 4

3 large squid, about 180g each, cleaned, with tentacles

few thyme sprigs, leaves stripped

few rosemary sprigs, leaves stripped

½ tsp coriander seeds, lightly crushed

1 small red chilli, sliced on the diagonal

2 garlic cloves, peeled and sliced

finely pared zest of 1 lemon

juice of 1½ lemons

3–4 tbsp olive oil, to drizzle

280g jar roasted peppers, drained

2 x 400g tins cannellini beans, rinsed and drained

sea salt and black pepper

small bunch of flat leaf parsley, chopped

To prepare the squid, cut along one side of the body pouches to open them out, then lightly score the flesh in a criss-cross pattern. Lay the scored squid and tentacles in a wide, shallow dish and sprinkle with the herb leaves, coriander seeds, chilli, garlic, lemon zest and the juice of 1 lemon. Drizzle over 2–3 tbsp olive oil and toss the squid to coat all over with the marinade. Cover with cling film and leave to marinate in the fridge for 20–30 minutes.

Heat the barbecue or a griddle pan. Transfer the squid to a plate, ready to cook, scraping off and reserving the excess marinade.

Pat the roasted peppers with kitchen paper to absorb excess oil, then slice into strips. Heat the reserved marinade from the squid in a sauté pan and add the peppers, beans, remaining lemon juice and some seasoning. Sauté for 3–5 minutes to heat through. Set aside.

Place the squid on the barbecue or griddle pan, laying the scored pieces flat. Cook until the squid turns opaque, about 1 minute on each side for the scored pieces, a little longer for the tentacles. Remove to a plate. When cool enough to handle, slice the squid body into strips and cut the tentacles in half.

Stir the sliced squid and chopped parsley through the warm peppers and beans. Serve immediately.

Grilled sardines with chermoula

a healthy boost of omega-3 fatty acids

Serves 4

8 very fresh sardines, gutted and cleaned

sea salt and black pepper

little olive oil, to drizzle

Chermoula:

2 tsp cumin seeds

2 tsp coriander seeds

2 garlic cloves, peeled and roughly chopped

1 tsp sweet paprika

finely grated zest and juice of 1 small lemon

4–5 tbsp extra virgin olive oil

small handful of coriander, chopped

To make the chermoula, toast the cumin and coriander seeds in a pan over a low heat until fragrant. Tip into a mortar and add a pinch each of salt and pepper. Grind to a fine powder, then add the garlic and grind the mixture to a paste. Stir in the rest of the ingredients.

Score the sardines lightly on both sides at 1cm intervals and place in a shallow dish. Pour half of the chermoula mixture over the fish and rub the marinade into the scored skin. Cover with cling film and leave to marinate in the fridge for at least 1 hour, or up to 4 hours.

Heat the barbecue or the grill to high. Season the sardines with a little salt and pepper and oil lightly. Place them in a sandwich-style wire barbecue rack, or on a wide oiled baking tray if grilling. Barbecue for 3 minutes each side, or grill for 4–5 minutes each side, basting with the pan juices as you turn them halfway.

Transfer the sardines to a warm platter, spoon over the remaining chermoula and serve with saffron rice pilaf or zesty couscous.

Spelt focaccia with rosemary and garlic

Serves 6

15g fresh yeast or 7g fast-action dried yeast

250ml lukewarm water

200g spelt flour

200g Italian '00'grade flour, plus extra to dust

1 tsp fine sea salt, plus extra to sprinkle (optional)

2 tbsp chopped rosemary leaves, plus extra whole leaves for sprinkling

6–7 garlic cloves, 2 peeled and finely crushed, the rest in their skins

about 50ml extra virgin olive oil, plus extra to drizzle

If using fresh yeast, put 2–3 tbsp of the lukewarm water in a small bowl and crumble in the yeast. Stir to dissolve and leave for about 10–15 minutes to foam.

Sift the flours and salt together into a large bowl, tipping in the bran left in the sieve. If using fast-action dried yeast, add it at this stage. Stir in the chopped rosemary.

Make a well in the centre. Add the crushed garlic, then pour in the yeast liquid (if using fresh yeast), olive oil and most of the remaining water. Stir with a wooden spoon until the mixture comes together. Add the rest of the water as necessary, a little at a time, to form a soft but not sticky dough.

Press the dough together then tip it onto a lightly floured surface. Knead for about 5 minutes to form a smooth, elastic dough. Place in a lightly oiled large mixing bowl, cover with a clean tea-towel and leave to rise in a warm spot for about 2 hours until the dough has doubled in size.

Heat the oven to 200°C/Gas 6. Turn the dough onto a lightly floured surface and knead lightly. Place on a well-oiled baking sheet and gently flatten with the palms of your hands. Pull and shape it towards the edges of the baking sheet to form a 1cm thick rectangle, about the size of an A4 sheet of paper. Press with your fingertips to create indentations in the dough.

Stud the dough randomly with rosemary leaves and whole garlic cloves and drizzle over a little olive oil. If you wish, sprinkle over a little sea salt. Bake for 15–20 minutes until golden brown. Leave to cool slightly. Slice and serve while still warm, with barbecued fish or meat.

lightly spiced and enhanced with a zingy salsa

Tandoori poussins
with mango relish

4 poussins, about 400–500g each

Tandoori marinade:

1 tsp ground turmeric

2 tsp garam masala

1 tsp ground coriander

1 tsp ground cumin

1 large garlic clove, peeled and finely crushed

3cm knob of fresh root ginger, peeled and finely grated

juice of ½ lemon

100ml natural yoghurt

small handful of coriander stalks, finely chopped

sea salt and black pepper

Mango relish:

1 firm but ripe mango

1 large red onion, peeled and finely chopped

1 red chilli, deseeded and finely chopped

juice of ½ lime

To spatchcock the poussins hold one, breast side down, on a chopping board. Using a pair of kitchen scissors, snip along both sides of the backbone to remove it. Turn the poussin over and press firmly down the middle with the palm of your hand to flatten it. Cut off the wing tip and trim off the excess skin and fat. Repeat with the remaining birds.

For the marinade, mix all the ingredients together in a large shallow bowl. Add the poussins and turn them over so that each bird is well coated. Cover with cling film and leave to marinate in the fridge for several hours, or preferably overnight.

Heat the oven to 170°C/Gas 3. Transfer the poussins to a large baking tray, pour on the marinade from the bowl and sprinkle with some salt and pepper. Cover with foil and bake for 30–40 minutes until just cooked through. To test, prick the thickest part of each poussin with a skewer and press gently – the juices should run clear. Take off the foil and set aside to cool.

Make the mango relish in the meantime. Peel the mango and chop the flesh, discarding the stone. Place in a bowl with the onion, chilli and lime juice. Toss to mix and season with salt and pepper to taste. Cover with cling film and chill for 20 minutes.

Heat the barbecue or a griddle pan until hot. Cook the poussins for 8–10 minutes, turning them over halfway, until nicely charred on both sides. Rest for a few minutes before serving, with the mango relish on the side.

Beef burgers with beetroot relish and cucumber raita

600g good quality lean beef mince

1 tsp smoked paprika

pinch of cayenne pepper

sea salt and black pepper

olive oil, to cook and drizzle

250g cherry tomatoes on the vine

splash of balsamic vinegar

4 Iceberg lettuce leaves, trimmed to neaten (optional)

handful of wild rocket leaves (optional)

Beetroot relish:

250g cooked beetroot in natural juices, drained

3 tbsp capers, rinsed and drained

handful of flat leaf parsley, roughly chopped

2 tbsp balsamic vinegar

3 tbsp olive oil

Cucumber raita:

1 large cucumber

handful of mint leaves, chopped

3–4 tbsp natural yoghurt

squeeze of lemon juice, to taste

Put the beef mince into a large bowl and add the paprika, cayenne, ½ tsp salt (or less to taste) and ½ tsp pepper. Mix well with your hands, then shape into 4 neat patties. Place on a plate or tray, cover with cling film and chill for at least 30 minutes to set the shape.

Make the beetroot relish in the meantime. Roughly chop the beetroot and place in a food processor along with the capers, parsley, balsamic vinegar and olive oil. Pulse until the mixture is roughly chopped – you don't want to purée the beetroot. Season to taste and transfer to a bowl.

For the cucumber raita, peel the cucumber and quarter lengthways. Scrape out the seeds with a spoon and discard. Roughly chop the flesh and place in a bowl. Add the chopped mint and toss with enough yoghurt to bind. Add the lemon juice and season with salt and pepper to taste.

Heat the barbecue or heat a little olive oil in a non-stick frying pan. Brush the burgers with olive oil and cook on the barbecue, or pan-fry allowing 3½–4 minutes on each side for medium burgers. Remove to a warm plate and leave to rest for a few minutes. Add the tomatoes to the barbecue or pan and drizzle with a little olive oil and balsamic vinegar. Cook for 1–2 minutes until the tomatoes are soft but still retain their shape.

Serve the burgers with the tomatoes, beetroot relish and cucumber raita. For a neat presentation, spoon the raita into lettuce cups and garnish with a handful of rocket.

Lamb kebabs with peppers and tomatoes

Serves 4

500g lean lamb leg steaks

1 large red pepper

1 large yellow pepper

8 chestnut mushrooms

8 cherry tomatoes, skinned if preferred

olive oil, to drizzle

Herb paste:

finely grated zest and juice of 1 lemon

2 garlic cloves, peeled and finely chopped

½ tsp dried oregano

½ tsp dried mint

½ tsp dried thyme

¼ tsp dried ground rosemary

½ tsp dried tarragon

1 tbsp olive oil

sea salt and black pepper

Cut the lamb steaks into 2.5cm cubes and place in a bowl. Stir together all the ingredients for the herb paste and pour over the lamb. Toss well to coat the pieces evenly. Cover the bowl with cling film and leave to marinate in the fridge for several hours, or overnight. Soak 6–8 bamboo skewers in cold water for least 20 minutes.

Halve the peppers, remove the core and seeds, then cut into 2.5cm pieces. Thread the peppers, lamb, mushrooms and cherry tomatoes alternately onto the soaked bamboo skewers.

Heat the barbecue or place a griddle pan over a high heat. Drizzle a little olive oil over the skewers and sprinkle with some salt and pepper. Barbecue or grill the skewers for 2½–3 minutes on each side. Leave to rest for a minute or two, then serve with side salads of your choice.

succulent, lean lamb marinated in a herb paste

5 ways with tomatoes

Mass-produced tomatoes picked before they've had a chance to ripen are usually tasteless. Vine-ripened tomatoes at their peak are altogether different. Recently, I visited an amazing organic farm in Wales. There must have been more than 20 different varieties of tomatoes slowly ripening on the vines. I was wide-eyed like a child in a candy store, taking in the varied colours and shapes of this versatile fruit.

Tomatoes are incredibly good for you. They are a useful source of nutrients, including vitamin C and beta-carotene, which the body converts to vitamin A. Probably their greatest asset, though, is the powerful antioxidant lycopene, which helps to protect the body from disease. Vine-ripened tomatoes are staples in our home kitchen – finding their way into salads, sauces and all manner of cooked dishes.

1 Mixed tomato salad

Use 1kg mixed vine-ripened tomatoes (including some cherry tomatoes). Halve or quarter the larger ones and place in a large bowl with the cherry tomatoes. Add 2 sliced spring onions and a handful of torn basil leaves. Dress with a squeeze of lemon juice, a drizzle of olive oil and some seasoning. **Serves 4–6**

2 Pasta with quick tomato sauce

Boil 300g dried penne in a pot of salted water until al dente. Meanwhile, in a blender, whiz 6 ripe plum tomatoes, 2 chopped garlic cloves, a chopped knob of ginger, 2 tbsp cider vinegar or lemon juice, 1 tbsp brown sugar, 1 tbsp tomato purée and the stalks from a handful of coriander until smooth. Tip into a saucepan, season and simmer for 5 minutes.

Drain the pasta, toss with a little olive oil and divide between warm bowls. Spoon over the tomato sauce and scatter with coriander leaves. **Serves 4**

124

3 Chunky gazpacho

Finely chop 6 ripe plum tomatoes, 1 small red onion, 1 red pepper and ½ cucumber (peeled and deseeded). Place in a large bowl, add a crushed garlic clove and sprinkle over the juice of ½–1 lemon, to taste. Season with salt and pepper and stir well. Pour over 300ml cold chicken or vegetable stock and 300ml tomato juice to cover, then stir in a dash each of Tabasco and Worcestershire sauce and some chopped basil and tarragon. Cover with cling film and chill for at least 4 hours to allow the flavours to develop. Serve in chilled bowls. **Serves 4**

4 Stuffed beef tomatoes

Heat oven to 200°C/Gas 6. Put 100g couscous in a heatproof bowl with a pinch each of saffron strands, salt and pepper. Pour on 125ml boiling hot chicken stock or water, cover and leave for 5 minutes.

Cut off the top third of each of 4 large beef tomatoes; reserve. Scoop the seeds into a bowl. Scoop out the flesh to hollow out the tomatoes, chop it finely and add to the seeds with a chopped handful each of coriander and mint, 3 sliced spring onions, the juice of ½–1 lemon, 30g toasted pine nuts, 30g sultanas and 2–3 tbsp olive oil. Mix well and season to taste.

Fluff up the couscous with a fork and stir in the tomato seed mixture. Spoon into the tomato shells and top with the lids. Place on a lightly oiled baking tray and bake for 15–20 minutes until soft. **Serves 4**

5 Homemade ketchup

Skin and chop 500g ripe plum tomatoes. Heat 1 tbsp olive oil in a saucepan and sweat 1 chopped sweet onion with 2 chopped garlic cloves over a medium-low heat for 4–6 minutes until softened. Lightly crush ½ tsp each fennel and coriander seeds and add to the vegetables with some seasoning. Cook, stirring, for half a minute, then add the chopped tomatoes, 300ml tomato juice or water, 50g light brown sugar, 1 tbsp red wine vinegar and a few basil sprigs. Simmer gently for 25–30 minutes or until the mixture is thick and the tomatoes are soft and pulpy. Adjust the seasoning and sweetness, adding a little more sugar or vinegar if needed. Whiz in a food processor or blender to a smooth purée, then pass through a fine sieve into a bowl and leave to cool. **Makes about 300ml**

Four cabbage coleslaw

low in calories and cholesterol, high in fibre

Serves 4

¼ Chinese cabbage

¼ Savoy cabbage

¼ white cabbage

¼ red cabbage

handful of chives, finely snipped

Dressing:

3 tbsp extra virgin olive oil

1 tbsp sesame oil

2 tbsp balsamic vinegar

2 tbsp wholegrain mustard

sea salt and black pepper

Cut out the core from each cabbage, then finely shred the leaves with a sharp knife. Place in a large bowl and toss well to mix.

For the dressing, whisk all the ingredients together in a bowl, seasoning with salt and pepper to taste. Pour over the shredded cabbage and toss to mix. Leave to marinate for at least 20 minutes before serving.

Scatter the chives over the coleslaw and toss to mix just before serving.

Fennel, pea and broad bean salad

Serves 4

2 medium fennel bulbs

4 large eggs, at room temperature

250g podded broad beans

250g podded peas, thawed if frozen

olive oil, to drizzle

8 Parma ham slices

Dressing:

1 small garlic clove, peeled and finely crushed

1 tsp caster sugar, or to taste

1 tbsp lemon juice

1 tbsp wholegrain mustard

3 tbsp extra virgin olive oil

handful of dill, roughly chopped

sea salt and black pepper

Trim the fennel, cutting off the base and removing the coarse outer layer of leaves. Cut each bulb in half lengthways, then slice as thinly as possible, using a mandolin or a sharp knife. Place in a large bowl of iced water and leave to soak for about 10–15 minutes to crisp up.

Meanwhile, add the eggs to a pan of simmering water and simmer for 9 minutes (the yolks should be set but still quite soft). Immediately drain, then refresh in a pan of cold water.

Bring another pan of water to the boil. Add the broad beans and blanch for 1 minute, then add the peas and return to the boil. Blanch for another 3 minutes until the peas and broad beans are tender. Drain and refresh in a bowl of iced water.

For the dressing, whisk all the ingredients together in a bowl, seasoning with salt and pepper to taste.

Add the broad beans and peas to the fennel. Pour over the dressing and toss well. Shell the eggs, then cut into quarters lengthways.

When ready to serve, heat a tiny drizzle of olive oil in a non-stick pan and fry the Parma ham slices until golden brown and crisp, turning once. Divide the salad and eggs between serving plates. Break the crispy Parma ham into smaller pieces and scatter over the salads. Sprinkle with pepper and serve.

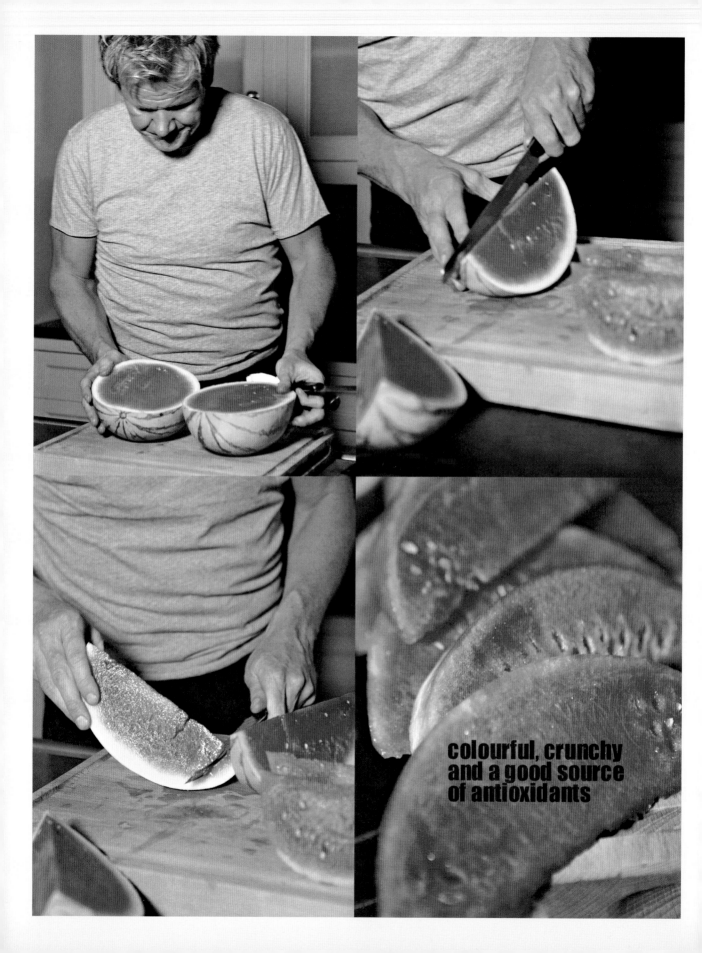

colourful, crunchy and a good source of antioxidants

Prawn, feta and watermelon salad

Serves 4

200g raw prawns, peeled and deveined

2 tbsp olive oil

pinch of cayenne pepper

sea salt and black pepper

1.5kg ripe seedless watermelon

50g wild rocket leaves, washed

120g feta cheese

1 tbsp toasted mixed seeds, such as pumpkin and sunflower seeds

Dressing:

2 tbsp lime juice

½ tsp caster sugar

4 tbsp extra virgin olive oil

Marinate the prawns by tossing them together with 1 tbsp olive oil, a pinch of cayenne and some salt and pepper in a bowl. Cover with cling film and leave to marinate in the fridge for 10–15 minutes.

Cut the watermelon into wedges, then cut off the skin and slice the flesh thinly. Layer the watermelon slices on a large serving platter, interleaving them with rocket leaves. Crumble over the feta and grind over some black pepper.

Place a large frying pan, preferably a non-stick one, over a medium heat and add 1 tbsp olive oil. Tip in the prawns and fry for about 2 minutes until they turn opaque, flipping them over after a minute or so. Transfer to a plate and leave to cool slightly while you make the dressing.

Whisk the dressing ingredients together and season to taste. Add the prawns to the platter and scatter over the seeds, if using. Drizzle with the dressing and serve at once.

Beetroot, carrot and chicory salad
with pomegranate dressing

loaded with vitamins, minerals and antioxidants

Serves 4

3 heads of chicory

2 medium carrots

250g cooked beetroot in natural juices

handful of toasted hazelnuts, lightly crushed (optional)

Dressing:

1 pomegranate

1 orange

2 tbsp balsamic vinegar

3–4 tbsp extra virgin olive oil

sea salt and black pepper

Trim the chicory, cutting off the base, then shred the leaves into matchsticks. Peel the carrots and cut them into ribbons, using a swivel vegetable peeler. Mix the chicory and carrot ribbons together in a salad bowl. Roughly cut the beetroot into quarters and add to the bowl.

For the dressing, halve the pomegranate and scoop out the seeds and juice into a bowl, picking out and discarding any membrane. Similarly, cut the orange in half and squeeze the juice into the bowl. Add the balsamic vinegar, olive oil and seasoning to taste. Blitz the mixture using a hand-held stick blender (or free-standing blender) until the pomegranate seeds are finely crushed. Pass the mixture through a fine sieve, pressing down on the pulp with the back of a spoon.

Spoon the dressing over the salad (any extra will keep in the fridge for a few days). Scatter a handful of toasted hazelnuts over the salad to serve if you like.

Baked stuffed figs
with goat's cheese and pine nuts

a fantastic way to finish a barbecue

Serves 4

8 ripe figs

100g soft goat's cheese

handful of chives, finely snipped

good quality balsamic vinegar, to drizzle

few thyme sprigs, leaves stripped

2 tbsp toasted pine nuts

Trim off the tip from each fig, then cut a cross through the top, cutting about halfway down. Squeeze the base of the figs to open out the top quarters like a flower.

Stuff the figs with the goat's cheese, sprinkle with snipped chives and drizzle with balsamic vinegar. Scatter over the thyme leaves and pine nuts.

Stand the figs on a large piece of foil. Bring up the sides and fold together to seal the parcel. You can either bake the figs in a hot oven, preheated to 200°C/Gas 6, or on a barbecue. They should take about 10–12 minutes. Unwrap the parcel and serve immediately, as a starter, an accompaniment or to round off a meal.

omega-3 boost

Oily fish are an excellent source of omega-3 fatty acids, which offer several health benefits. Studies have indicated a lower incidence of cardiovascular disease among those who consume oily fish regularly. It is thought that these essential fatty acids improve the flow of blood through smaller blood vessels, helping to reduce the chances of blood clots, and ultimately, the risk of strokes and heart attacks. Omega-3's also have anti-inflammatory properties. There is some evidence to suggest that they may improve brainpower and concentration, too. Certainly these fatty acids are important for healthy brain and nerve development, so they are particularly valuable for children and pregnant mums.

Other sources of omega-3 fatty acids include linseed, walnuts and walnut oil. However, oily fish is deemed to be the richest source.

Eating oily fish more often – ideally once or twice a week – is the best way to obtain your omega-3's. Don't get yourself into a rut, though. Try a different type of fish each time and vary the way you cook and serve them. Of course they are delicious simply grilled or pan-fried with the minimum of oil and served with a tomato or leafy salad to cut the richness, but you can also turn these fish into tasty pâtés (see page 170). And don't forget to opt for the sustainable varieties, such as trout, bream, sardines, mackerel and herrings.

Healthy suppers

Fish cakes with anchovy dressing

Serves 4

400g La Ratte, Charlotte or other waxy potatoes

2 tbsp olive oil

finely grated zest of 1 large lemon

2–3 tbsp lemon juice

sea salt and black pepper

few thyme sprigs

½ lemon, sliced

300g salmon fillet

300g smoked haddock fillet

handful of flat leaf parsley, chopped

handful of chervil, chopped

3 tbsp plain flour

2 medium eggs, lightly beaten

50g Japanese panko breadcrumbs

2 tbsp olive oil

Anchovy dressing:

2 tbsp capers

2 shallots, peeled and finely chopped

bunch of flat leaf parsley, leaves only, chopped

4 marinated anchovies, chopped

4 tbsp extra virgin olive oil

Peel the potatoes, cut into even-sized pieces and drop into a pan of well salted water. Bring to the boil and cook for 10–15 minutes until tender when pierced with a knife. Drain well. While still hot, mash the potatoes using a potato ricer back into the pan. Mix in the olive oil, lemon zest, lemon juice and seasoning to taste. Leave to cool.

Meanwhile, add the thyme, lemon slices and salmon to a wide pan of slowly simmering salted water and poach for a minute. Slide in the smoked haddock and gently poach for another 4–5 minutes until both fish are almost cooked through. Transfer to a plate, using a fish slice. When cool enough to handle, break the fish into large flakes, discarding the skin and any pin-bones.

Mix the fish and chopped herbs into the mashed potatoes, using your hands. Taste and adjust the seasoning. Divide the mixture into four and shape into neat patties. Season the flour with salt and pepper. Coat the fish cakes in seasoned flour, then dip into the egg and finally into the breadcrumbs, turning to coat evenly all over. Reshape them as necessary and place on a tray or plate. Chill for 2 hours to set the shape.

To cook, heat the oven to 180°C/Gas 4. Heat a thin layer of olive oil in a wide ovenproof frying pan. Fry the fish cakes for 2–3 minutes until golden brown, then flip over and fry the other side for 1–2 minutes. Finish cooking in the oven for 5–7 minutes.

Make the dressing in the meantime, by gently warming all the ingredients together in a pan for 3–4 minutes. Spread a generous spoonful of dressing on each warm plate and rest a fishcake in the centre. Serve immediately, with peas or beans.

Glazed ling with sweet 'n' sour shallots

Serves 4

4 skinless ling fillets, about 170g each

a little olive oil, for oiling

60ml light soy sauce

2 tbsp dark soy sauce

100ml white wine vinegar

50g soft brown sugar

1 tsp coriander seeds, lightly crushed

1 tsp black peppercorns, lightly crushed

3cm knob of fresh root ginger, peeled and finely grated

400g small shallots, peeled

75ml dry white wine

150ml fish stock (see page 248)

small handful of chives, snipped

Lay the fish fillets in a lightly oiled large baking dish and set aside. Put the soy sauces, wine vinegar and sugar in a saucepan and stir over a low heat to dissolve the sugar. Increase the heat and tip in the coriander seeds, peppercorns and ginger. Boil for 8–10 minutes until the liquid has reduced by half. Leave to cool completely.

Heat the oven to 180°C/Gas 4. Blanch the shallots in a pan of boiling water for 10 minutes until tender, then drain.

Pour the soy mixture over the ling fillets and cook in the oven for 5 minutes until the sauce begins to caramelise. Scatter the blanched shallots around the fish and pour on the white wine and fish stock. Return to the oven and bake for another 6–8 minutes until the fish is just cooked through.

Transfer the fish to a warm plate, using a fish slice. Cover with foil and set aside to rest in a warm place for 5–10 minutes. Meanwhile, tip the onions and liquor into a pan and boil for 10 minutes until reduced to a sticky sauce.

Place the fish on warm plates and spoon over the shallots and sauce. Garnish with snipped chives and serve with steamed rice and stir-fried pak choi, if you wish.

Note If you are unable to find ling fillets, you can use cod or whiting instead.

rich in protein, low in fat

Spiced monkfish
with crushed potatoes, peppers and olives

Serves 4

4 monkfish tail fillets, skinned, about 170g each

1 tsp five-spice powder

1 tsp sweet paprika

1 tsp salt

2 tbsp olive oil

handful of flat leaf parsley, chopped

lemon wedges, to serve

Crushed potatoes:

750g new potatoes, scraped clean

sea salt and black pepper

2 tbsp extra virgin olive oil

squeeze of lemon juice

200g drained roasted peppers in oil (from a jar), chopped

75g pitted black olives, roughly chopped

handful of basil leaves, shredded

Heat the oven to 200°C/Gas 6. Next, to cook the potatoes, add them to a pan of well salted boiling water and cook for about 10–15 minutes until tender.

Lay the monkfish on a board and remove any greyish membrane. Mix the five-spice powder, paprika and salt together on a plate. Roll the monkfish fillets in the spice mixture to coat evenly all over. Place a roasting pan in the oven to heat up.

Heat the olive oil in a heavy-based frying pan and sear the monkfish fillets, in batches if necessary, for 1½–2 minutes on each side until golden brown all over. Transfer the monkfish fillets to the hot roasting pan and bake for 8–10 minutes until the fish is just cooked through. When ready, remove from the oven, cover with foil and leave to rest for 5 minutes.

Drain the potatoes as soon as they are done and return to the pan. Lightly crush them with the back of a fork or a potato masher and mix in the extra virgin olive oil, lemon juice and some seasoning. Stir in the chopped peppers, olives and basil. Taste and adjust the seasoning.

Cut the monkfish into thick slices. Spoon the crushed potatoes onto warm serving plates and arrange the monkfish on top. Sprinkle with the chopped parsley and serve at once, with lemon wedges and spinach or broccoli.

Seared yellowfin tuna with black beans

flavourful protein-packed meal

Serves 4

4 yellowfin tuna steaks, about 200g each and 2cm thick

sea salt and black pepper

1 tsp coriander seeds, lightly crushed

1½–2 tbsp olive oil

Black beans:

200g black beans, soaked overnight

few thyme sprigs

1 bay leaf

1 onion, peeled and halved

1 carrot, peeled and cut into 3 chunks

3–4 tbsp olive oil

2 red onions, peeled and finely chopped

1 garlic clove, peeled and finely chopped

6 spring onions, trimmed and finely sliced

handful of coriander leaves, chopped

juice of ½ lemon juice, or to taste

Cook the beans first. Drain, then tip into a large pan and add the thyme, bay leaf, onion and carrot. Pour in enough water to cover by 3–4cm. Bring to a simmer and cook for 40–50 minutes until the beans are soft. Fish out the herbs, carrot and onion and discard. Drain the beans and leave to cool.

Heat a frying pan and add 3 tbsp olive oil. Tip in the red onions and garlic and cook, stirring frequently, for 4–6 minutes until they begin to soften but not brown. Stir in the black beans and cook for a few minutes to warm through. Use a fork to roughly mash the beans in the pan or gently pound with the end of a rolling pin – leaving some whole for a varied texture. If the mixture looks dry, add another 1 tbsp olive oil and a splash of water, then mix through the spring onions, coriander and lemon juice. Season with salt and pepper to taste. Keep warm while you cook the tuna.

Season the tuna with salt and pepper and coat one side of the steaks with the crushed coriander seeds. Heat a frying pan, add the olive oil and pan-fry the steaks for 2 minutes on each side. Transfer to a warm plate, cover with foil and leave to rest for a few minutes.

Divide the beans between warm serving plates and lay the tuna steaks on top. Serve at once.

Herby crayfish
and prawn pilaf

plenty of essential minerals and B vitamins

2–3 tbsp olive oil

3 small or 2 large red onions, peeled and thinly sliced

250g basmati rice

finely pared zest of 2 lemons

few thyme sprigs

2 garlic cloves (unpeeled), lightly smashed

sea salt and black pepper

550ml hot fish stock (see page 248)

750g live crayfish, washed

250g large raw prawns

handful of chives, finely snipped

handful of basil leaves, finely sliced

handful of chervil leaves, roughly chopped

Heat the oven to 190°C/Gas 5. Cut a greaseproof paper circle slightly larger than a heavy-based ovenproof pan or a cast-iron casserole. Snip a small hole in the middle of the paper to act as a steam vent.

Heat the pan with the olive oil, then sauté the onions for 4–6 minutes until they begin to soften. Stir in the rice, lemon zest, thyme, garlic and some seasoning. Stir well to toast the rice for a couple of minutes. Pour in the hot fish stock and bring to the boil. Add the crayfish to the pan and quickly cover with the greaseproof paper. Transfer the pan to the oven.

After 15 minutes, take the pan out of the oven, lift the greaseproof paper and scatter over the prawns. Re-cover with the greaseproof paper and return to the oven for 10 minutes until the rice is tender and the prawns are just cooked through and opaque. Remove from the oven and leave to stand for about 5 minutes before lifting off the paper.

Fork through the rice to distribute the shellfish evenly. Check the seasoning and stir in the chopped herbs. Serve at once.

Steamed prawns
with black bean sauce

Serves 4

500g large raw prawns

5–6 Chinese cabbage leaves

sea salt

2 spring onions, trimmed

Sauce:

1½ tbsp sunflower oil

1 large garlic clove, peeled and finely crushed

3cm knob of fresh root ginger, peeled and finely crushed

pinch of dried chilli flakes

1½–2 tbsp fermented black beans (available from Asian food stores)

75ml chicken stock (see page 249)

2 tbsp light soy sauce

2 tbsp rice wine

1 tbsp mirin

2 tsp caster sugar, or to taste

1 tsp cornflour, mixed with 1 tbsp water

First, make the sauce. Heat the oil in a pan and add the garlic, ginger, chilli flakes and black beans. Stir-fry for a couple of minutes, then pour in the stock, soy sauce, rice wine and mirin. Bring to a simmer, then stir in the sugar and cornflour mixture. Simmer for a few minutes, stirring frequently, until the sauce has thickened. Pour into a wide bowl and leave to cool.

Peel the prawns and devein them, by cutting a slit along the back and removing the dark thread. Bring a large pan of water (that will hold a large steamer basket) to the boil. If you don't have a steamer, overturn a heatproof bowl in a large pan or wok (with lid) and pour in enough hot water to come halfway up the sides of the bowl. Bring to a simmer.

Blanch the cabbage leaves in boiling salted water for 2–3 minutes. Drain well and use to line a large, shallow heatproof bowl (that will fit in the steamer), trimming the edges of the leaves as necessary.

Arrange the prawns on the cabbage and spoon the sauce over them. Place in the steamer and cook for 8–9 minutes until the prawns are just firm and opaque. Meanwhile, finely slice the spring onions on the diagonal.

Scatter the spring onions over the prawns and serve immediately, with steamed rice and stir-fried vegetables if you wish.

Thai-style beef stir-fry

Serves 4

400g beef fillet, trimmed and cut into thin strips

1 garlic clove, peeled and chopped

2cm knob of fresh root ginger, peeled and chopped

½ red chilli, trimmed and roughly sliced

150g chestnut mushrooms, trimmed and thinly sliced

1 carrot, peeled and thinly sliced on the diagonal

1 red pepper, cored, deseeded and sliced into thin strips

150g mangetout

2 spring onions, trimmed and sliced on the diagonal

sea salt and black pepper

3 tbsp sunflower oil

handful of Thai sweet basil (or coriander) leaves, to garnish

Sauce:

2 tbsp light soy sauce

3 tbsp oyster sauce

1 tbsp rice vinegar

1 tsp caster sugar

1 tsp cornflour

3–4 tbsp water

Have the beef and all the aromatic ingredients and vegetables chopped and ready before you begin to cook.

For the sauce, mix all the ingredients together in a small bowl and set aside. Lightly season the beef strips with salt and pepper.

Heat a wok or a large frying pan until hot then add a little oil, swirling the wok to coat the surface evenly. Add half the beef strips and stir-fry for about a minute until just brown on the surface, but still medium rare in the middle. Remove to a plate and repeat with the remaining beef. Set the beef aside.

Add a little more oil to the wok along with the garlic, ginger and chilli. Stir-fry the mixture for about a minute until lightly golden and fragrant. Toss in the mushrooms and stir-fry for a minute. Add the carrot and a splash of water. (This will create steam, to help cook the vegetables evenly.) After a minute, toss in the red pepper and mangetout. Stir-fry for another 2 minutes or until the vegetables are just tender.

Give the sauce a stir and pour over the vegetables, then return the beef to the wok. Toss over the heat for another minute until the sauce has thickened. Turn off the heat and stir in the spring onions.

Spoon the stir-fry onto warm serving plates and scatter over the basil leaves. Serve at once, with steamed jasmine rice.

Vietnamese beef and noodle soup

Serves 4

500g beef fillet

2.5cm knob of fresh root ginger, peeled and finely grated

1 large garlic clove, peeled and finely crushed

sea salt and black pepper

1 tbsp sesame oil, plus extra to toss

200g dried thin rice noodles

150g bean sprouts

2–3 spring onions, trimmed and thinly sliced on the diagonal

small bunch of coriander, leaves only

small bunch of mint or Thai sweet basil, leaves only

Broth:

1.5 litres beef stock (see page 249)

4cm knob of fresh root ginger, peeled and thinly sliced

4 star anise

3 cloves

2 cinnamon sticks

1 cardamom pod, lightly crushed

2 tsp caster sugar, or to taste

3 tbsp fish sauce

To serve:

lime wedges

hoisin sauce

Vietnamese chilli sauce

Trim the beef of any sinew, then slice as thinly as possible. Place in a bowl and add the grated ginger, garlic, some pepper and the sesame oil. Toss to mix, cover and leave to marinate in the fridge for 30–40 minutes.

For the broth, pour the beef stock into a large pan and add the rest of the ingredients with a little salt and pepper. Bring to the boil, lower the heat and simmer for about 30 minutes. Strain the broth into a clean pan, discarding the ginger and spices. Taste and adjust the seasoning.

Add the rice noodles to a large pan of boiling salted water and cook according to the packet instructions until tender, but still retaining a bite. Drain in a colander and immediately toss the noodles with a little sesame oil to prevent them from sticking.

Bring the broth to the boil and tip in the beef and bean sprouts. Simmer for just 30 seconds, then remove from the heat.

Divide the noodles among warm bowls and ladle the hot broth over them, dividing the beef and bean sprouts equally. Scatter over the spring onions, coriander and mint. Serve immediately, with lime wedges and little individual dishes of hoisin and Vietnamese chilli sauces for dipping.

Spiced pork chops
with sweet potatoes

Serves 4

4 pork loin chops with bone, about 300g each

½–1 tsp mild chilli powder, to taste

1 tsp sweet paprika

sea salt and black pepper

2 tbsp olive oil

few thyme sprigs

4 garlic cloves (unpeeled), lightly smashed

5–6 star anise, lightly smashed

1 tsp coriander seeds, lightly crushed

3 large sweet potatoes, about 350g

1 red chilli, trimmed, deseeded and finely chopped

bunch of coriander, chopped

Cut off the rind and excess fat around the pork chops. Mix the chilli powder, paprika and some salt and pepper with the olive oil in a wide baking dish. Add the thyme, garlic, star anise and coriander seeds. Add the pork chops and turn to coat. Cover and leave to marinate for at least 30 minutes, or in the fridge overnight.

Heat the oven to 180°C/Gas 4. Bake the pork chops, uncovered, for about 15 minutes until the meat is just firm when lightly pressed.

Meanwhile, bring a pan of salted water to the boil. Peel the sweet potatoes and cut into 1½cm slices. Add to the pan and cook for 7–8 minutes until almost tender when pierced with a skewer. (They should be slightly undercooked at this stage.) Drain and refresh under cold running water. Dice the potatoes; set aside.

When cooked, transfer the chops to a warm plate, cover with foil and rest in a warm place for 10 minutes. Squeeze out the soft garlic from the skins and return to the baking dish. Add the chilli, tip in the sweet potatoes and toss to mix. Season lightly and bake for 10 minutes, stirring once or twice, until the potatoes are tender.

Stir the coriander through the sweet potatoes and spoon onto warm plates. Add a pork chop to each plate and serve.

Braised pork with leeks and pak choi

plenty of protein and B vitamins

Serves 4

600g pork tenderloin

2 tbsp olive oil

sea salt and black pepper

1 large leek, white part only, thinly sliced

3cm knob of fresh root ginger, peeled and cut into matchsticks

3–4 garlic cloves, peeled and chopped

400ml water

200ml dry white wine or rice wine

2–3 tbsp light soy sauce, to taste

1½ tbsp caster sugar, or to taste

2 large heads of pak choi, about 250g

Cut the pork into bite-sized chunks, trimming away any fat or sinew. Heat a cast-iron or heavy-based frying pan with a little olive oil. Lightly season the pork pieces and fry in batches for about a minute on each side, until golden brown all over. Remove to a plate and set aside.

Add a little more oil to the pan and stir in the leek, ginger and garlic. Stir frequently over a medium-high heat for 4–6 minutes until the leek begins to soften. Add the water, wine, soy sauce and sugar, scraping the bottom of the pan with a wooden spoon to deglaze.

Return the pork to the pan and stir well. Bring to the boil, then reduce the heat to a simmer. Partially cover the pan with a lid and gently braise for an hour, stirring from time to time, until the pork is very tender and the sauce has reduced by half.

Cut the pak choi into quarters lengthways and place on top of the pork. Cover the pan with the lid and cook for another 3–4 minutes until the pak choi is just tender. Serve the braised pork and vegetables with steamed rice.

Stuffed chicken breasts wrapped in sage and Parma ham

Serves 4

4 large chicken breasts, about 170–200g

8 sage leaves

5 heaped tbsp ricotta

sea salt and black pepper

8 Parma ham slices

1½ tbsp olive oil

handful of thyme sprigs

Cut a deep slit along one side of each chicken breast, without slicing right through, then open it out like a book. On a clean chopping board, finely chop 4 sage leaves, then mix into the ricotta and season with salt and pepper to taste.

Lay two Parma ham slices on the board, overlapping them slightly. Put a sage leaf in the middle and lay an open chicken breast on top. Spoon a quarter of the ricotta mixture onto the middle of the chicken, then fold the sides together again, to enclose the filling. Now wrap the Parma ham slices around the stuffed chicken breast. Wrap in cling film. Repeat with the rest of the chicken breasts and chill for 1–2 hours to firm up slightly.

Heat the oven to 180°C/Gas 4 and place a roasting pan in the oven to heat up. Heat a heavy-based frying pan and add the olive oil. When hot, fry the Parma-wrapped chicken, in batches if necessary, for 2 minutes on each side until browned. Lay a few thyme sprigs on each chicken breast, then place in the hot roasting pan. Cook in the oven for 12–15 minutes, depending on size, or until the meat feels just firm when lightly pressed.

Rest the chicken, covered with foil, in a warm place for 5–10 minutes. Slice each stuffed breast thickly on the diagonal and arrange on warm plates. Serve with steamed greens and light mashed potatoes or a zesty couscous.

Conchiglie with lamb ragù

Serves 4

3 tbsp olive oil

500g lean minced lamb

sea salt and black pepper

1 large onion, peeled and finely chopped

2 garlic cloves, peeled and chopped

1 celery stick, finely chopped

1 large carrot, peeled and finely chopped

1 tbsp tomato purée

1 rosemary sprig, leaves only, chopped

few sage leaves, chopped

125ml dry white wine

700g passata

250ml hot water

pinch of sugar (optional)

300g dried conchiglie (shells) or other pasta shapes

Heat a large non-stick frying pan and add 1 tbsp olive oil. When hot, add the lamb mince and some seasoning. Fry, stirring occasionally, for 8–10 minutes until evenly browned. Tip into a colander set over a large bowl to drain off the excess oil.

Meanwhile, heat the remaining oil in a large cast-iron pan. Add the onion, garlic, celery and carrot and cook, stirring, over a high heat for 4–6 minutes until lightly golden brown. Stir in the tomato purée and cook for another 2 minutes. Add the chopped herbs and pour in the wine, stirring and scraping the bottom of the pan to deglaze. Let the wine simmer until it has reduced to a syrupy glaze.

Add the browned lamb, passata and hot water. Stir well and bring to a low simmer. Partially cover the pan with a lid and simmer for 1–1½ hours until the lamb is tender, giving the mixture a stir every now and then. Taste and adjust the seasoning, adding a pinch of sugar if necessary to balance the acidity of the tomatoes. (If preparing in advance, the ragù can now be cooled down and chilled or frozen.)

When ready to serve, bring a pot of salted water to the boil. Add the pasta and boil according to the packet instructions, until al dente. Drain and immediately toss with a drizzle of olive oil. Divide between warm bowls and spoon over the lamb ragù to serve.

Calves liver with caramelised onions

liver is rich in iron and B vitamins

Serves 4

350g calves liver

1 heaped tbsp plain flour

sea salt and black pepper

1–2 tbsp olive oil

small handful of flat leaf parsley, chopped

Caramelised onions:

2 sweet onions, peeled and thinly sliced

2 tbsp olive oil

pinch of caster sugar

splash of balsamic vinegar

Lemon polenta:

200g instant polenta

550ml whole or semi-skimmed milk

550ml chicken stock (see page 249)

2 tbsp crème fraîche

finely grated zest of 1 lemon

2 tbsp lemon juice, or to taste

Cook the onions first. Heat the olive oil in a pan and add the onions with a little seasoning. Cover and sweat for 6–8 minutes, stirring occasionally, until soft. Remove the lid and increase the heat. Stir in the sugar and cook, stirring frequently, until the onions are golden brown. Add a splash of balsamic vinegar and let bubble until well reduced and the pan is quite dry. Keep warm.

Make the polenta next. Heat the milk and stock in a large saucepan with some seasoning. When it begins to simmer, gradually add the polenta, whisking constantly to prevent lumps forming. Simmer and stir for about 5 minutes. Take off the heat and stir in the crème fraîche, lemon zest and juice. Check the seasoning. Cover and keep warm while you prepare the liver.

Trim the liver, peeling away the membrane if necessary. Cut into 1cm thick slices, prising out larger tubes with the knife tip. Mix the flour with a pinch each of salt and pepper on a plate. Lightly coat the liver slices in the seasoned flour.

Cook the liver in batches. Heat a large non-stick frying pan over a high heat. Add the olive oil, then fry a few slices of liver for about 40 seconds on each side until nicely browned, but still pink in the middle. Remove to a warm plate and repeat to cook the rest, adding a little more oil if needed.

Give the polenta a stir and spoon onto warm plates. Top with the caramelised onions and pan-fried liver. Sprinkle over some chopped parsley and serve at once.

Baked courgette
and wild mushroom
risotto

Serves 4

4 courgettes

sea salt and black pepper

2 large garlic cloves, peeled and thinly sliced

few basil sprigs, leaves only

2–3 tbsp olive oil, plus extra to drizzle

squeeze of lemon juice

550–600ml vegetable or chicken stock (see pages 248–9)

200g risotto rice such as Carnaroli, Arborio or Vialone Nano

100ml dry white wine

200g wild mushrooms, cleaned and halved or sliced if large

2–3 tbsp finely grated Parmesan

Heat the oven to 200°C/Gas 6 and line a large baking tray with foil. Halve the courgettes lengthways and score the flesh in a criss-cross pattern. Arrange cut side up on the tray. Season lightly and scatter over the garlic slices and basil leaves. Drizzle with olive oil and squeeze over a little lemon juice. Bake for 30–40 minutes until the courgettes are soft. Let them cool slightly, then roughly chop the flesh.

For the risotto, bring the stock to a simmer in a pan. Heat another medium saucepan and add 1 tbsp olive oil. Stir in the rice and cook, stirring, for a minute. Pour in the wine and let it bubble to reduce down until the pan is quite dry. Gradually add the stock, a ladleful at a time, stirring frequently. Let the rice absorb most of the stock in the pan before adding another ladleful.

When the rice is al dente, stir in the chopped courgettes and turn off the heat. Leave the risotto to stand for a few minutes.

Meanwhile, heat a wide frying pan and add 1–2 tbsp olive oil. Tip in the mushrooms, season and toss over a high heat for 3–4 minutes until they are golden brown and any moisture released has been cooked off. Mix the mushrooms into the risotto, adding a little more boiling stock if you prefer a 'wet risotto'. Stir in most of the Parmesan and adjust the seasoning.

Divide the risotto among warm plates and sprinkle over the remaining Parmesan to serve.

Grilled provençal vegetable salad

serve with couscous, or as a side dish with grilled fish or meat

Serves 4

1 large courgette, trimmed

1 medium aubergine, trimmed

1 red pepper

1 yellow pepper

2 garlic cloves, peeled and finely crushed

1 tsp herbes de Provence

2 tbsp olive oil

sea salt and black pepper

1 tbsp balsamic vinegar

extra virgin olive oil, to drizzle

1–2 tbsp toasted pine nuts

few basil leaves, torn

Cut the courgette and aubergine into ½cm thick slices. Halve, core and deseed the peppers, then cut into slices and place in a bowl with the other vegetables.

Stir the garlic, herbs, olive oil and seasoning together in a bowl. Drizzle over the vegetables and toss well to coat.

Heat a large griddle or heavy-based frying pan until hot. Griddle the vegetables until they are tender, basting frequently and turning halfway through cooking. The peppers and courgettes will take about 4–5 minutes; the aubergines will need 6–8 minutes.

Arrange the vegetables on a warm serving platter and drizzle over the balsamic vinegar and extra virgin olive oil. Scatter over the pine nuts and torn basil. Serve warm or at room temperature.

Braised aubergines
Szechuan-style

Serves 4

2 medium aubergines, trimmed

4 tbsp sunflower oil

3cm knob of fresh root ginger, peeled and finely chopped

2 garlic cloves, peeled and finely chopped

1 large onion, peeled and roughly chopped

1 red chilli, trimmed, deseeded and finely chopped

1 red pepper, cored, deseeded and chopped

sea salt and black pepper

2 spring onions, trimmed and thinly sliced on the diagonal

1 tbsp toasted sesame seeds, to garnish

Sauce:

150ml vegetable or chicken stock (see pages 248–9)

2 tbsp light soy sauce

2 tbsp rice wine

2 tsp Worcestershire sauce

2 tsp caster sugar, or to taste

1½ tsp cornflour

Cut the aubergines into 1½cm slices, then halve the slices to give half-moons.

For the sauce, mix all the ingredients together in a small bowl and set aside.

Heat a large pan and add half the oil. Tip in the ginger, garlic, onion and chilli and stir-fry over a medium heat for 4–5 minutes until the onion begins to soften. Stir in the red pepper and cook for another minute before adding the remaining oil and the aubergine pieces. Season lightly and cook, turning frequently, for 3–4 minutes.

Give the sauce a stir and pour into the pan. Stir well, then turn the heat to low. Simmer for 8–10 minutes or until the aubergines are just tender, giving the mixture a stir every now and then.

Transfer to a serving dish and scatter over the spring onions and sesame seeds. Serve with bowls of steamed rice or Oriental noodles.

Penne primavera

delicately flavoured spring vegetables and pasta

Serves 4

300g dried penne or other pasta shapes

sea salt and black pepper

8–10 baby leeks, white part only

4 baby fennel, trimmed

8 radishes, trimmed and halved lengthways

6 baby carrots, scrubbed or peeled

4 baby turnips, scrubbed and halved

4 baby courgettes, trimmed and thickly sliced on the diagonal

few thyme sprigs

3–4 tbsp extra virgin olive oil

juice of ½ lemon

handful of basil leaves, shredded

handful of mint leaves, shredded

3–4 tbsp freshly grated Parmesan, to serve (optional)

For the pasta, bring a pot of salted water to the boil. At the same time, bring a large pan of water (that will take a large steamer basket) to the boil ready to steam the vegetables. Put all the baby vegetables into your steamer basket and sprinkle over the thyme sprigs and a little sea salt.

Set the steamer basket over the pan of boiling water. Cover and steam for 6–8 minutes until the vegetables are just tender.

Meanwhile, add the pasta to the boiling salted water and cook until al dente, according to the packet instructions. Reserving a little water in the pan, drain the pasta into a colander then tip back into the pan and immediately toss with the olive oil and lemon juice.

When cooked, add the vegetables to the pasta, discarding the thyme sprigs. Toss to mix and season well to taste. Mix through the shredded herbs and divide between warm serving plates. Serve as is, or with a sprinkling of grated Parmesan.

Moroccan spiced pumpkin and butter bean pot

Serves 4

1kg wedge of cooking pumpkin (about 750g peeled weight)

4 tbsp olive oil

1 banana shallot (or 3 regular ones), peeled and chopped

2 garlic cloves, peeled and finely chopped

sea salt and black pepper

1 tsp paprika

1 tsp ground ginger

1 tsp ground cumin

1 tsp ground turmeric

500–600ml hot chicken stock (see page 249)

2 x 400g tins butter beans, rinsed and drained

bunch of flat leaf parsley, chopped

bunch of coriander, chopped

4 tbsp natural or Greek yoghurt, to serve

Remove the skin from the pumpkin, discard the seeds and roughly chop the flesh into 5cm cubes. Heat half the olive oil in a large saucepan and add the pumpkin, shallot, garlic and some seasoning. Stir over a high heat for 10 minutes until the pumpkin cubes are lightly caramelised and soft. Add the spices and stir over the heat for another couple of minutes.

Pour in the stock to cover the pumpkin and bring to a simmer. Cook for 10 minutes, then remove from the heat and leave to cool slightly. While still hot, purée the mixture in a blender until smooth and creamy. (You may need to do this in two batches.)

Return the purée to the pan and bring to a simmer. Tip in the butter beans and chopped herbs. Place over a medium heat for 2–3 minutes until the beans are hot. Taste and adjust the seasoning.

Ladle the soup into warm bowls and add a spoonful of yoghurt. Serve with plenty of warm flat breads.

Note For a lighter version of this soup, as illustrated, use one tin of butter beans rather than two.

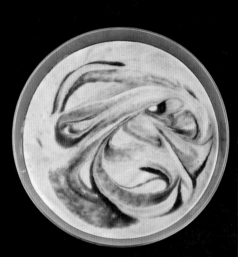

Healthy kids

Lunchbox dips and dunkers

Serves 4–6

Smoked mackerel pâté:

250g smoked mackerel fillets

2 tbsp horseradish cream

5 tbsp reduced-fat crème fraîche

2 tbsp lemon juice, or to taste

freshly ground black pepper

Minted chickpea purée:

400g tin chickpeas, rinsed and drained

4 tbsp natural yoghurt

2 tbsp lemon juice, or to taste

sea salt and black pepper

handful of mint leaves, chopped

To serve:

raw vegetable sticks, such as carrots, celery, cucumber, red and yellow peppers

cooked shelled prawns tossed with a drizzle of olive oil and thyme (optional)

To make the fish pâté, flake the smoked mackerel, checking for pin-bones, and place in a food processor. Pulse a few times to break the fish apart. Add half the horseradish cream, crème fraîche, lemon juice and some black pepper (you won't need to add salt) and pulse again until smooth. Taste the mixture and add more horseradish cream, crème fraîche and lemon juice until you are happy with the flavour and seasoning. Spoon the mixture into a lunchbox or plastic container and chill.

For the chickpea purée, put the chickpeas, yoghurt, lemon juice and some seasoning into a food processor. Blend until smooth. Transfer the mixture to a bowl and taste for seasoning, adding more lemon juice, salt and pepper as necessary. Stir through the chopped mint and chill in a lunchbox or plastic container.

Pack a selection of raw vegetable sticks in a separate container to serve with the dips. If liked, pack some prawns in another container. Add some breadsticks or pita bread, too. Follow with fresh fruit or yoghurt.

Note The lunch must be packed in an insulated cooler bag with ice blocks to keep it chilled, especially if prawns are included.

a balanced lunch to keep kids
nourished and sustained

Crusted fish fillets
with tomato ketchup

a healthy alternative to fish fingers

Serves 4

4 thick, skinless cod fillets, about 130–140g each

50g fresh white breadcrumbs

finely grated zest of 1 lemon

25g Parmesan, freshly grated

1–2 thyme sprigs, leaves stripped

sea salt and black pepper

1–2 tbsp olive oil

lemon wedges, to serve

homemade ketchup (see page 125)

Heat the oven to 220°C/Gas 7. Check the cod fillets carefully for pin-bones, removing any that you come across with kitchen tweezers. Place the fillets, skinned side up, on a lightly oiled baking tray.

In a bowl, mix together the breadcrumbs, lemon zest, Parmesan, thyme and a little salt and pepper to taste. Stir in a little olive oil to combine.

Spread the breadcrumb mixture evenly on top of each fish fillet. Bake in the oven for 7–8 minutes until the topping is golden brown and crisp, and the fish flesh is opaque.

Transfer the fish to warm plates and add a lemon wedge, for squeezing. Serve with homemade ketchup, mash and peas or broccoli.

Turkey brochettes
with red pepper salsa

skinless turkey breast is one of the leanest meats you can buy

Serves 4–5

500g skinless, boneless turkey breasts

sea salt and black pepper

2 red onions, peeled

1 yellow pepper

1 orange pepper

olive oil, to brush

Marinade:

1 tbsp lime juice

1 tbsp olive oil

½ tsp smoked paprika

½ tsp celery salt

½ tsp cornflour

pinch of cayenne pepper

dash of Tabasco sauce (optional)

dash of Worcestershire sauce

Red pepper salsa:

250g jar roasted red peppers in olive oil

1 small red onion, peeled and finely chopped

4 spring onions, trimmed and finely chopped

handful of coriander leaves

juice of 1 lime

½ tsp honey, to taste

Cut the turkey into 2.5–3cm cubes. Whisk together all the ingredients for the marinade in a large bowl, adding some salt and pepper. Add the turkey and toss well to coat. Cover with cling film and leave to marinate in the fridge for at least 30 minutes or overnight. Soak 4–5 bamboo skewers in cold water for least 20 minutes.

Cut the onions into bite-sized chunks, similar in size to the turkey cubes. Halve, core and deseed the peppers, then cut into 2.5–3cm squares. Thread the peppers, onions and turkey cubes alternately onto the skewers. Place on a lightly oiled tray, cover with cling film and chill until ready to cook.

For the salsa, drain the peppers and chop finely. Place in a bowl and add all the rest of the ingredients. Toss together and season with salt and pepper to taste. (The salsa is now ready to eat, or it can be chilled for up to an hour.)

To cook, heat a griddle pan or the grill until hot. Brush the brochettes with a little olive oil and cook for 10–15 minutes, turning several times. The turkey should feel just firm when lightly pressed; don't overcook or it will be dry. Serve immediately, with the red pepper salsa.

Chicken burgers
with sweet potato wedges

low fat burger and chips

Makes 6 small burgers

3 tbsp olive oil

1 medium sweet onion, peeled and finely chopped

2 garlic cloves, peeled and finely crushed

sea salt and black pepper

350g minced skinless, boneless chicken breasts

1 large egg

handful of herbs, such as flat leaf parsley and chives, chopped

Sweet potato wedges:

3 medium sweet potatoes, peeled

olive oil, to drizzle

honey, to drizzle (optional)

To serve:

6 mini buns, preferably wholemeal, split

1 large ripe avocado

squeeze of lemon juice

1 large beef tomato, thinly sliced

homemade ketchup (see page 125)

Heat 1 tbsp olive oil in a pan and sweat the onion and garlic with some seasoning for 4–6 minutes until soft but not brown. Tip into a large bowl; leave to cool completely.

Add the chicken, egg and seasoning, then stir in the chopped herbs, until evenly distributed. Cover with cling film and chill for an hour to allow the mixture to firm up.

Shape the mixture into 6 small patties, with moist hands; try not to compact them. Place on a tray lined with baking parchment. Chill until ready to cook.

Heat the oven to 200°C/Gas 6. Line a baking tray with baking parchment. Cut the sweet potatoes into wedges and place in a large bowl with a drizzle of olive oil and some seasoning. Spread out in a single layer on the baking tray and bake for 15–20 minutes until golden brown at the edges. If you wish, drizzle with a little honey. Keep warm in a low oven.

To cook the burgers, heat 2 tbsp olive oil in a large frying pan or griddle pan. When hot, add the patties and fry for 4 minutes on each side until golden brown and just cooked through. (Don't press them with a spatula as they cook or you'll squeeze out the juices.) Remove to a warm plate and leave to rest.

Lightly toast the buns on both sides. Halve, peel and stone the avocado, then slice thinly, squeezing over a little lemon juice to prevent them discolouring. Sandwich each bun with a chicken burger and a few slices of avocado and tomato. Serve immediately, with the sweet potato wedges and ketchup.

Stir-fried duck
in lettuce cups

Serves 4–6

1 Iceberg lettuce

4 duck breasts, about 175g each

¼ tsp Szechuan peppercorns

½ tsp black peppercorns

½–1 tsp five-spice powder

pinch of sea salt

olive oil, to drizzle

1 cucumber

2 spring onions, trimmed

5–6 tbsp hoisin sauce

1 tbsp sesame seeds, to sprinkle

For the lettuce cups, remove the outer layers from the lettuce until you get 4–6 neat whole leaves. Trim around each leaf with scissors to neaten the edges, so that they resemble cups. Place one on each serving plate.

Remove the skin and fat from the duck breasts, then slice the flesh into thin strips. Put the peppercorns, five-spice powder and sea salt into a mortar and grind to a powder. Sprinkle this over the duck slices, drizzle with a little olive oil and toss to coat evenly.

Halve the cucumber and scoop out the seeds, then cut the flesh into finger-length strips. Slice the spring onions very finely on the diagonal.

Heat a non-stick wide frying pan until hot and you can feel the heat rising above the pan. Add the duck and stir-fry for 2 minutes. Add the spring onions and hoisin sauce and toss well to coat. Stir-fry for another minute until the duck is just cooked through. Toss with a handful of cucumber strips.

Divide the stir-fry between the lettuce cups. Sprinkle with the sesame seeds and scatter the remaining cucumber strips around each plate. Serve immediately.

Rigatoni with yellow and green courgettes

Serves 4–5

250g dried rigatoni or other pasta shapes

sea salt and black pepper

2 large green courgettes, trimmed

2 large yellow courgettes, trimmed

3–4 tbsp olive oil

1 garlic clove, peeled and finely crushed

handful of basil leaves

Parmesan, to grate

Add the pasta to a pot of boiling salted water and cook according to the packet instructions until al dente.

Meanwhile, halve the courgettes lengthways and slice thickly. Heat a large frying pan and add the olive oil. Tip in the crushed garlic and sauté for just less than a minute.

Add the courgettes with a pinch of salt and a grinding of pepper. (If your pan is not large enough, cook the courgettes in two batches.) Fry over a high heat for 3–4 minutes until the courgettes are just tender and lightly golden brown around the sides. Take off the heat.

When ready, drain the pasta and immediately toss with the courgettes and basil. Taste and adjust the seasoning. Divide among warm plates and grate over some Parmesan to serve.

Baked eggs
with ratatouille

eggs are one of the best sources of protein for children

Serves 4

1 large red onion, peeled

1 small aubergine, trimmed

1 large red pepper, halved, cored and deseeded

1 large green pepper, halved, cored and deseeded

1 large courgette, trimmed

3–4 tbsp olive oil

sea salt and black pepper

2 garlic cloves, peeled and finely chopped

1/4–1/2 tsp mild chilli powder (optional)

1 tsp ground cumin

1 tsp sweet paprika

250g tinned chopped tomatoes

4 large eggs

Heat the oven to 200°C/Gas 6. Chop the onion, aubergine, peppers and courgette into 1.5cm cubes, keeping them separate. Put a large frying pan over a high heat and add the olive oil, onion and a little seasoning. Sauté for 2 minutes, then add the aubergines, peppers and garlic and fry for another minute. Tip in the courgettes and sauté for another minute or two.

Add the ground spices and chopped tomatoes. Bring to a simmer and cook for 8–10 minutes until the vegetables are tender. Taste and adjust the seasoning.

Divide the ratatouille between four individual shallow ovenproof dishes. Make an indentation in each portion with the back of a spoon, then crack an egg into each one. Sprinkle the top of each egg with a pinch each of salt and pepper.

Stand the dishes on a large baking tray and bake for 10–12 minutes until the egg whites are set but the yolks are still runny in the middle. Serve immediately, with some wholemeal toasts on the side.

181

Fromage frais, yoghurt and plum purée ripple

plenty of protein and calcium for strong bones and teeth

Serves 4–6

4 ripe plums, about 500g

½ tsp ground cinnamon

2–3 tbsp caster sugar, to taste

1 star anise (optional)

300ml low-fat natural yoghurt

300ml reduced-fat fromage frais

2–3 tbsp icing sugar, or to taste

Halve the plums, remove the stones and roughly chop the flesh. Toss with the cinnamon and 2 tbsp caster sugar. Place a wide frying pan over a high heat, tip in the plums and add the star anise if using. Sauté for 4–6 minutes until the plums are soft, moistening with a splash of water if necessary. Taste for sweetness, adding more sugar if the plums are too tart. Discard the star anise.

Transfer the cooked plums to a blender or food processor and whiz until smooth. For a really smooth purée, pass through a fine sieve to remove any pulpy bits. Leave to cool completely.

Spoon the yoghurt and fromage frais into a large bowl and add the icing sugar. Beat lightly to mix, then ripple through all but 2 tbsp of the plum purée. Spoon into individual glasses or plastic tumblers and swirl the remaining plum purée on top. Serve at once.

Healthy entertaining

Mixed fish sashimi

serve as an elegant starter, or cocktail party food

Serves 4–6 as a starter

400g sashimi-grade swordfish fillet

400g sashimi-grade centre-cut tuna fillet

300g sashimi-grade skinless salmon fillet

1 very fresh mackerel, about 300g, filleted (optional, see note)

To serve:

light soy sauce

pickled ginger

wasabi paste

Trim off any dark flesh from the swordfish and neaten the edges (you can save all the fish trimmings to make fishcakes). Trim the tuna to a neat log and neaten the edges of the salmon fillet. Carefully check over the salmon and mackerel fillets for pin-bones, removing any you find with kitchen tweezers.

Wrap each fish in cling film and place in the freezer for 45 minutes to allow the flesh to firm up slightly, making them easier to slice.

Take the fish from the freezer and remove the cling film. Thinly slice each fish with a very sharp knife and overlap the fish slices in neat rows on a serving platter. The sashimi can now be chilled for a few hours until ready to serve. Bring to the table with little dipping bowls of light soy sauce, pickled ginger and wasabi paste.

Note Only use mackerel if you are able to obtain a freshly caught fish from the sea. Otherwise, use an extra 100g each swordfish, tuna and salmon.

5 ways with leafy greens

The diversity of greens is astonishing. As a child, I ate lots of kale, which was, and still is, regarded as a humble vegetable, akin to swede and turnip. But like spinach and the once exotic cavalo nero, kale is fantastic in soups and stews, or simply sautéed with a touch of garlic and chilli.

The general rule is the darker the colour, the richer the nutrients. In addition to fibre, leafy veg provide calcium, magnesium, iron, zinc, folic acid and the valuable antioxidants – beta-carotene and vitamin C. These are important for boosting the immune system and improving digestion. So, aim to eat a variety of leafy greens through the week, making the most of what is in season.

1 Bruschetta with cavalo nero and Parma ham

Chop 2 bunches (300–350g) of cavalo nero. Cook 8 slices of Parma ham in a large non-stick frying pan until brown and crisp on both sides. Transfer to a plate; set aside. Add 2 tbsp olive oil to the pan and 4 unpeeled garlic cloves. Fry for a minute or two to flavour the oil, then add the cavalo nero, some seasoning and a glass of water. Cook, stirring frequently, for 5–6 minutes until the leaves are tender and the water has cooked off. Meanwhile, halve a ciabatta lengthways, then cut each piece in two and toast lightly. Pile the ham and cavalo nero onto the warm toasts and serve, topped with the garlic. **Serves 4**

2 Purple sprouting broccoli with Thai flavours

Cut 400g purple sprouting broccoli into even lengths. For the dressing, mix 1 deseeded, finely chopped small red chilli with 2 tbsp sesame oil, 1½ tbsp fish sauce, the juice of 1 lime and ½–1 tsp caster sugar. Cook the broccoli in a steamer for 4 minutes until tender and bright green. As soon it is cooked, transfer to a warm plate and spoon over the dressing. Sprinkle with 1 tbsp toasted sesame seeds and serve immediately. **Serves 4**

3 Spinach with chickpeas and harissa

Drain a 400g can of chickpeas, rinse in a sieve and set aside to drain. In a large frying pan, fry 2 chopped garlic cloves in 2 tbsp olive oil over a low heat, without browning. Tip in the chickpeas, add 1 tbsp harissa and some seasoning and increase the heat slightly. Stir and cook for 3–4 minutes until the chickpeas are warmed through. Stir in 200g baby spinach leaves and cook for barely a minute just until the spinach has wilted. Transfer to warm plates and serve immediately. **Serves 2**

4 Pak choi with ginger and garlic

Wash 500g pak choi and separate the stalks and leaves, then slice the stalks on the diagonal into bite-sized pieces. Chop 1 large garlic clove and a 2cm knob of fresh root ginger. Heat a wok until hot, then add 1½ tbsp groundnut oil, followed by the garlic and ginger. Stir-fry for a minute, adding the pak choi stalks with a small splash of water as the garlic and ginger begin to colour. Add the leaves, 2 tbsp oyster sauce and a few grindings of black pepper. Stir-fry over a high heat for another 30 seconds until the pak choi is tender. Transfer to a warm plate and serve. **Serves 4**

5 Kale, chorizo and potato soup

Trim 200g kale, cutting off the hard stems, then finely chop the leaves and place in a bowl; set aside. Heat 2 tbsp olive oil in a large pan and sauté 2 chopped onions and 2 finely chopped garlic cloves for 5–6 minutes, stirring frequently, until soft but not browned. Tip in 150g diced chorizo sausage, stir and fry for a few more minutes.

Add 2 diced, scrubbed, large red-skinned potatoes, 1.5 litres water to cover, and some salt and pepper. Stir well and bring to the boil. Lower the heat and simmer for 10–12 minutes until the potatoes are just cooked. Tip in the kale and simmer for another 3–5 minutes until it is tender. Check the seasoning and serve in warm bowls. **Serves 4**

Hot and sour clam broth with noodles

delicate flavours, high in nutrients, yet low in fat

Serves 4–6 as a starter

Broth:

5cm knob of fresh root ginger, peeled and sliced into matchsticks

1 lemongrass stalk, trimmed and chopped

2 red chillies, trimmed and sliced

4–5 kaffir lime leaves

3 tbsp fish sauce

3 tbsp rice wine vinegar

3 tbsp light soy sauce

2½ tbsp palm sugar or soft brown sugar

juice of 1 lime

1.5 litres fish stock (see page 248)

To serve:

1.2kg fresh clams

600g fresh udon noodles

sesame oil, to drizzle

handful of basil or coriander leaves, torn

Put all the ingredients for the broth into a large pan and bring to the boil, stirring occasionally to help dissolve the sugar. Reduce the heat slightly and simmer for 3–4 minutes. Bring another pan of water to the boil for the noodles.

Scrub the clams under cold running water and discard any that do not close tightly when tapped. Increase the heat under the broth pan and slide the clams into the broth. Cover, bring back to the boil and simmer for 3–4 minutes until the shells have opened. Discard any that remain shut.

Meanwhile, add the noodles to the pan of boiling water and cook for about 2 minutes, then tip into a colander and drain well. Immediately toss with a drizzle of sesame oil and divide among warm bowls. Ladle over the clams and hot broth. Scatter over some torn basil or coriander and serve.

Chilled leek and avocado soup

Serves 4 as a starter

2 tbsp olive oil

250g leeks, white part only, finely chopped

1 onion, peeled and finely chopped

sea salt and black pepper

splash of dry white wine

1 medium potato, about 150g, peeled and chopped

bouquet garni (thyme sprig, bay leaf and a few parsley stalks, tied together)

750ml vegetable or chicken stock (see pages 248–9)

1 large ripe avocado

juice of ½ lemon, or to taste

Heat the olive oil in a large pan and add the leeks, onion and some seasoning. Stir, then cover and let the vegetables sweat over a low heat for 5 minutes until softened.

Remove the lid, turn up the heat slightly and add a splash of wine. Let bubble until reduced down to a syrupy glaze. Stir in the potato and add the bouquet garni. Pour in the stock and bring to the boil. Season with salt and pepper, then cover and leave to simmer for 10–15 minutes until the potato is soft. Discard the bouquet garni.

Halve the avocado, remove the stone and scoop out the flesh into a blender. Ladle in half of the soup liquor and vegetables and blend to a smooth purée. Tip into a large bowl, or for a really smooth soup, push the purée through a fine sieve into the bowl. Blend the remaining liquor and vegetables until smooth and add to the rest of the soup. Stir and adjust the seasoning, adding salt, pepper and a little lemon juice to taste.

Let the soup cool, then chill for a few hours or overnight. Pour into chilled bowls to serve.

Baby spinach, artichoke
and watercress salad

packed with vitamins and minerals

300g baby spinach leaves

200g watercress, trimmed of stalks

280g jar grilled artichoke halves in olive oil

1 unwaxed lemon, for zesting

Parmesan shavings, to serve

Dressing:

1 garlic clove, peeled

sea salt and black pepper

1 tbsp wholegrain mustard

1½ tbsp cider vinegar

4 tbsp extra virgin olive oil

2 tbsp walnut oil

For the dressing, finely crush the garlic with a pinch each of salt and pepper, using a large pestle and mortar. Stir in the mustard, cider vinegar, olive oil and walnut oil. Taste and adjust the seasoning.

Wash the spinach and watercress leaves, pat dry and place in a large salad bowl. Drain the artichoke hearts and pat with kitchen paper to absorb the excess oil. Cut each artichoke half in two and add to the salad leaves. Finely grate the zest from the lemon over the salad and add a handful of Parmesan shavings.

Toss the salad with the dressing just as you are ready to serve. Divide between serving plates and scatter over a few more Parmesan shavings if you wish.

Seared scallops
with minted peas and broad beans

Serves 4

24 king scallops, shelled and cleaned

coarse sea salt

250g podded peas, thawed
if frozen

300g podded broad beans, thawed
if frozen

2 thyme sprigs, leaves only

1–2 tbsp olive oil

small knob of butter

handful of mint, leaves roughly chopped

extra virgin olive oil, to drizzle

Take the scallops from the fridge and set aside while you cook the vegetables. Bring a pan of salted water to the boil, tip in the peas and blanch for 3–4 minutes or until tender. Scoop them out with a slotted spoon and plunge into a bowl of iced water to refresh. Drain well and tip into a bowl.

Return the water to the boil and blanch the broad beans for 3–4 minutes or until tender. Drain well, refresh in iced water and drain again. Gently squeeze the broad beans to pop them out of their skins. Add to the peas and set aside.

Put the thyme leaves on a board and sprinkle with 1 tsp coarse sea salt. Chop finely, then sprinkle the thyme salt over one side of the scallops. Heat a griddle or large frying pan and add the olive oil.

Pan-fry the scallops for 1½ minutes on each side, depending on thickness – they should feel slightly springy when pressed. Make sure you turn them in the same order you put them into the pan to ensure even cooking. Remove to a warm plate and rest for a minute while you reheat the vegetables.

Tip the peas and broad beans into the frying pan and add a splash of water and a little butter. Heat for a minute to warm through, season to taste and toss through the mint leaves.

Spoon the vegetables onto warm plates and top with the scallops. Sprinkle with a little more thyme salt if you wish. Drizzle a little extra virgin olive oil around each plate and serve immediately.

Red mullet
with orange and
fennel en papillote

Serves 4

8 red mullet fillets, about 100g each

2 large oranges

1 large or 2 medium heads of fennel

2 red chillies

2 tsp fennel seeds

olive oil, to drizzle

4 splashes of dry white wine

Heat the oven to 200°C/Gas 6. Cut 4 large squares of baking parchment. Fold each square in half to form a crease in the middle, then open out and set aside. Check the red mullet fillets for pin-bones, removing any with kitchen tweezers.

To prepare the oranges, slice off the top and bottom, then cut off the peel and pith following the curve of the fruit. Now, holding the orange over a sieve set on top of a bowl to catch the juice, cut along the membranes to release each segment. Squeeze out any juice from the pulp and discard.

Trim the fennel, then slice thinly. Halve, deseed and thinly slice the chillies into rings.

Divide the fennel slices, orange segments and chilli slices among the parchment squares, piling them on one side of the crease. Lay two red mullet fillets on each pile. Scatter over the fennel seeds and drizzle with a little olive oil. Fold the other side of the parchment over the filling to enclose.

To seal each parcel, make small folds all along the edges to hold them together. Just before the final fold, tilt the parcel slightly and pour in a splash of wine and a quarter of the orange juice. Repeat with the remaining parcels.

Place the parcels on two large baking sheets and bake for 10 minutes until the fish is just firm, opaque and cooked through. Put a parcel on each warm plate and bring to the table to cut open.

peppers are packed with
immune-boosting antioxidants

Saffron-marinated bream with sweet and sour peppers

Serves 4

4 black bream fillets, about 140g each

2½ tbsp olive oil

generous pinch of saffron strands

sea salt and black pepper

basil sprigs, to garnish

Sweet and sour peppers:

6 red peppers

2 tbsp olive oil

1 tsp caster sugar

small splash of red wine vinegar

Trim the bream fillets to neaten and pull out any pin-bones with kitchen tweezers. Mix the olive oil and saffron strands together in a wide dish. Add the fish fillets and toss well to coat. Grind over some pepper, cover with cling film and leave to marinate in the fridge for 20 minutes.

To prepare the peppers, halve, core and deseed, then cut into thin slices. Heat the olive oil in a large frying pan or wok, add the peppers and stir-fry over a high heat for 2–3 minutes until they begin to soften. Season with salt and pepper and add the sugar and a small splash of wine vinegar. Let bubble for a minute or two until the vinegar has cooked down and the peppers are tender. Take off the heat and set aside; keep warm.

To cook the fish, heat a wide non-stick frying pan until hot. Season the bream fillets with salt and pepper and fry, skin side down, for about 2 minutes until the skin is golden brown and crisp. Flip the fillets over and fry the other side for a minute until the flesh is opaque.

Divide the peppers between warm plates and top with the bream fillets. Serve immediately, garnished with basil.

Glazed salmon
with pak choi and shiitake

Serves 4

4 skinless salmon fillets, cut from the thick end, about 140g each

Marinade:

2 tbsp miso paste

1 tbsp mirin

½ tbsp sesame oil

½ tbsp sake

½ tbsp light soy sauce

1 tbsp caster sugar or honey

freshly ground black pepper

Pak choi and shiitake:

500g pak choi, washed and drained

200g shiitake mushrooms, cleaned and stalks removed

1 tbsp groundnut oil

1 garlic clove, peeled and finely chopped

finger-length knob of fresh root ginger, peeled and finely shredded

sea salt and black pepper

1 tbsp light soy sauce

1 tbsp fish sauce

2 tsp rice wine vinegar

1 tbsp sesame seeds, to sprinkle

Check the salmon fillets for pin-bones, removing any you find with kitchen tweezers. Mix all the marinade ingredients together in a small bowl to make a paste and spread this all over each fillet to coat. Place the fillets in a wide dish, cover with cling film and leave to marinate in the fridge for at least 30 minutes, preferably overnight.

Trim the pak choi, cutting off the base to separate the individual leaves. Cut off the green leaves and set aside; finely shred the stalks. Cut off the woody stalks from the shiitake mushrooms, then slice thickly.

Heat the oven to 220°C/Gas 7. Place the salmon fillets on a non-stick or lightly oiled tray and bake for 5–7 minutes until cooked around the edges but still medium rare in the centre. The fillets should feel slightly springy when pressed. Transfer to a warm plate and set aside to rest in a warm place.

Meanwhile, to cook the vegetables, heat the oil in a wok or large frying pan over a medium heat. Tip in the garlic and ginger and stir-fry for a minute until golden. Add the mushrooms, season lightly and stir-fry for about 2 minutes until any juices released have been cooked off. Add the pak choi leaves and stalks followed by the soy sauce, fish sauce and rice wine vinegar. Stir-fry for another minute until the pak choi has just wilted.

Pile the stir-fry onto warm plates. Break the salmon fillets into large flakes and arrange on top. Add a sprinkling of sesame seeds and serve, with bowls of steamed rice.

Stir-fried duck with noodles

quick and easy special stir-fry for two

Serves 2

2 skinless duck breasts, about 140g each, trimmed

1 garlic clove, peeled and finely grated

3cm knob of fresh root ginger, peeled and finely grated

1 tsp five-spice powder

sea salt and black pepper

3 tbsp oyster sauce

1 tbsp dark soy sauce

½ tsp cornflour, mixed with 2 tbsp water

2 portions of dried noodles, such as thin udon or Chinese egg noodles about 65g each

sesame oil, to drizzle

1–2 tbsp olive oil

1 long red chilli, trimmed and sliced on the diagonal

2 heads of pak choi, leaves separated

3 spring onions, trimmed and chopped

grated zest of 1 lime, plus a squeeze of juice

Slice the duck breasts thickly and toss with the grated garlic, ginger, five-spice powder and a little salt and pepper. Stir the oyster sauce, soy sauce and cornflour mixture together in a small bowl.

For the noodles, bring a pot of water to the boil. Add the noodles and cook for 2 minutes less than the suggested time (on the packet instructions). Drain well and immediately toss with a drizzle of sesame oil.

Heat a wok or large non-stick frying pan and add a little olive oil. When hot, add the duck fillets and fry over a high heat for 1–1½ minutes until golden brown around the edges but not completely cooked through. Remove to a plate and set aside.

Add a little more oil to the pan and tip in the chilli and pak choi. Stir-fry for a minute, then pour in the sauce mixture. Bring to a simmer, then return the duck to the pan and cook for another minute. The sauce should begin to thicken.

Add the noodles and spring onions to the pan. Toss over the heat until the noodles are warmed through. Squeeze over a little lime juice and serve immediately, sprinkled with grated lime zest.

lean, succulent white meat and quick-braised vegetables

Guinea fowl with pea and lettuce fricassée

Serves 4

4 boneless guinea fowl breasts, about 130g each

sea salt and black pepper

1½ tbsp olive oil

few thyme sprigs, plus extra to garnish

Pea and lettuce fricassée:

small knob of butter

500g podded peas, thawed if frozen

few thyme sprigs

splash of water or chicken stock (see page 249)

3–4 Iceberg lettuce leaves, shredded

Trim the guinea fowl breasts to neaten and season with a little salt and pepper. Heat a wide frying pan and add a little olive oil. Add the guinea fowl breasts, skin side down, with the thyme sprigs and fry for about 4–5 minutes until the skin is golden brown and crisp.

Turn the breasts and cook on the other side for about 2 minutes. They should feel very slightly springy when pressed and should be succulent and slightly pink inside. Transfer to a warm plate and set aside to rest in a warm place while you make the fricassée.

Melt the butter in a pan and tip in the peas with some seasoning. Add the thyme sprigs and a splash of water or stock and braise the peas for 3–4 minutes until tender and the pan is almost dry. Toss in the shredded lettuce and cook for another minute until the leaves have just wilted. Taste and adjust the seasoning.

Divide the fricassée among warm plates and rest a guinea fowl breast on top. Serve at once, garnished with thyme. Accompany with new potatoes if you like.

Honey-glazed partridge with bashed neeps and cabbage

Serves 2

2 oven-ready partridges, about 300g each

sea salt and black pepper

2 tbsp olive oil

6 garlic cloves (unpeeled)

few rosemary sprigs

few thyme sprigs

2–3 tbsp honey

Bashed neeps:

1 large swede, about 550g

15g butter

Sautééd cabbage:

½ head of Savoy cabbage, core removed and shredded

1½ tbsp olive oil

squeeze of lemon juice, to taste

For the bashed neeps, peel the swede and cut into 3–4cm chunks. Cook in salted water to cover for about 15 minutes until quite soft. Meanwhile, blanch the cabbage in another pan of salted water for 2–3 minutes. Drain and refresh under cold running water, then drain again and set aside.

Drain the swede and return to the pan. Add the butter and crush with a potato masher, seasoning with a little more salt and pepper to taste. (For a smooth mash, whiz in a food processor, then return to the pan.)

Season the partridges and heat up a frying pan. When hot, add the olive oil, garlic, rosemary and thyme. Sear the partridges for 1½–2 minutes on each side until nicely browned. Drizzle the honey over the birds and add a good splash of water to the pan. Cook, basting frequently, for 6–8 minutes until the partridge breasts feel slightly springy when pressed, indicating that they're medium rare. Transfer to a warm plate and rest for a few minutes while you reheat the vegetables.

Warm up the bashed neeps, giving the mixture a few stirs. For the cabbage, heat the olive oil in a pan, then add the blanched cabbage and toss until piping hot. Adjust the seasoning with salt, pepper and a little lemon juice.

Pile the bashed neeps and sautéed cabbage onto warm plates and sit the braised partridges alongside. Serve immediately.

Roasted pigeon
with pickled red cabbage

Serves 4

4 oven-ready wood pigeons, about 280g each

1½ tbsp olive oil

sea salt and black pepper

small knob of butter

Pickled red cabbage:

1 red cabbage, about 850g

30g butter

50g brown sugar

60ml red wine or malt vinegar

To prepare the cabbage, quarter and cut out the tough core, then finely shred the leaves and place in a bowl. Melt the butter in a large, wide pan and add the sugar and vinegar with a little splash of water. Stir until the sugar has dissolved, then add the shredded cabbage and toss to coat. Cover and braise for 45 minutes to 1 hour until the cabbage is tender, lifting the lid to give it a stir every once in a while.

Heat the oven to 190°C/Gas 5. (Aim to cook the pigeons about 20 minutes before the cabbage will be ready.) Heat a wide ovenproof pan and add a little olive oil. Season the pigeons inside and out with salt and pepper. Add to the hot pan and fry for about 2 minutes on each side until evenly browned all over. Add a knob of butter, turn the pigeons breast upwards and spoon the foaming butter over them to baste.

Transfer the pan to the oven and roast for another 8–10 minutes to finish cooking the pigeons – the breasts should feel slightly springy when pressed, indicating that they are medium-rare. Remove from the oven and rest in a warm place for 5–10 minutes.

To serve, pile the pickled red cabbage onto warm serving plates and place a roasted pigeon alongside.

packed with protein, iron and vitamin C

Pot-roast sirloin of beef with root vegetables

Serves 4

1.2kg beef sirloin

2–3 tbsp plain flour

sea salt and black pepper

2 large carrots, peeled and halved lengthways

1 swede, peeled

1 large kohlrabi, peeled

2 large leeks, trimmed

4 tbsp olive oil

1 head of garlic, halved horizontally

150ml red wine

300ml beef or chicken stock (see page 249)

handful of thyme sprigs

handful of rosemary sprigs

1 tsp black peppercorns

1 tsp coriander seeds

Heat the oven to 180°C/Gas 4. Trim off any excess fat and sinew from the beef. Mix the flour with a generous pinch each of salt and pepper on a wide plate. Roll the beef in the seasoned flour to coat, shaking or patting off any excess. Set aside.

Cut all the vegetables into large chunks. Put a large cast-iron casserole or heavy-based pan over a medium-high heat. Add a thin layer of olive oil and tip in the carrots, swede and a little seasoning. Fry for 4–5 minutes, stirring frequently, until golden brown. With a slotted spoon, transfer to a colander set over a large bowl to drain off any oil. Next, fry the kohlrabi, leeks and garlic, with a little more oil if necessary. Add to the colander.

Sear the beef in the hot pan, adding a little more oil if necessary, for 8–9 minutes until evenly browned all over. Transfer to a plate and set aside. Pour the red wine into the pan, stirring to deglaze, and let bubble until reduced by two-thirds. Stir in the stock. Return the beef and any juices released to the pan.

Spoon the vegetables around the beef and add the herbs, peppercorns and coriander seeds. Cover with a lid and transfer to the oven. Cook for about 25–30 minutes for medium-rare beef. Transfer the beef to a platter, cover with foil and leave to rest in a warm place for about 15 minutes.

Just before carving, spoon the vegetables onto a serving platter and keep warm. The sauce will be quite thin; to thicken it if required, boil to reduce slightly, then pass through a fine sieve into a warm jug. Thinly slice the beef and add to the platter. Serve with some rustic bread and a side salad if you wish.

Seared fillet of veal with Jerusalem artichoke purée

For the purée, put the Jerusalem artichokes into a pan with some salt and pepper and pour in the water or stock to cover. Bring to a simmer and cook for about 15–20 minutes until very soft. Drain the artichokes, reserving the cooking liquor.

Tip the artichokes into a food processor and add the butter. Blend for a few minutes until smooth, adding a splash of the liquor as necessary to get the right texture. You'll need to stop the machine to scrape down the sides once or twice. Push the purée through a sieve back into the pan and season well.

Heat the oven to 200°C/Gas 6. Cut any sinew off the veal and trim the edges to neaten so that the veal is evenly thick throughout. Rub all over with olive oil and season with salt and pepper. Heat a wide ovenproof frying pan until hot. Add a little oil to the pan and sear the veal fillet for about 2 minutes on each side until browned all over.

Transfer the pan to the oven and cook for 20 minutes or until the veal is medium rare – it should feel slightly springy when pressed. Transfer to a warm platter, cover with foil and rest for 5–10 minutes while you reheat the artichoke purée.

Carve the veal into thick slices and overlap them on warm serving plates. Pour any juices from the platter into the hot pan, then drizzle over each plate. Serve with the Jerusalem artichoke purée, and purple sprouting broccoli if you wish.

Serves 4

800g veal fillet

1½–2 tbsp olive oil

sea salt and black pepper

Artichoke purée:

600g Jerusalem artichokes, thinly sliced

500ml water or vegetable stock (see page 248)

small knob of butter

veal is low in fat, yet high in protein

Rump of lamb
with Puy lentils and green beans

Trim the lamb of any sinew, then place in a wide dish with the herbs, coriander seeds, peppercorns and olive oil. Toss to coat the meat and leave to marinate in the fridge for at least a few hours, preferably overnight.

To cook the lentils, put them in a saucepan with the herbs and garlic, then pour on the stock. Bring to the boil, lower the heat and simmer for 15–20 minutes until tender. Drain the lentils, reserving the stock; discard the garlic and herb sprigs.

Blanch the beans in a pan of salted water for 3–5 minutes until tender. Drain and refresh in a bowl of iced water, then drain again. Set aside.

Heat the oven to 190°C/Gas 5. Sprinkle the lamb with a little salt and sear in a hot ovenproof pan for 2–3 minutes. Turn over and cook the other side for 2 minutes until browned. Transfer the pan to the oven and roast for 6–8 minutes until medium rare – the lamb will be slightly springy when pressed. Transfer to a warm plate and pat with kitchen paper to absorb the excess fat. Cover with foil and leave to rest for 5 minutes.

Meanwhile, pour off most of the fat from the pan and tip in the lentils and beans. Add a splash of balsamic vinegar, a little of the reserved stock and some seasoning. Toss over a high heat for a few minutes to warm the beans and lentils through.

Spoon the lentils and bean onto warm serving plates. Thickly slice the lamb and arrange on top. Drizzle over any remaining pan juices and serve.

Serves 4

4 thick rumps of lamb, about 220g each

few thyme sprigs

few rosemary sprigs

1 tsp coriander seeds, lightly crushed

1 tsp black peppercorns, lightly crushed

1 tbsp olive oil

sea salt

Lentils and green beans:

250g Puy lentils

few thyme sprigs

few rosemary sprigs

½ head of garlic, cut horizontally

800ml chicken stock (see page 249)

300g green beans

splash of balsamic vinegar

energise... exercise

An active lifestyle has been important to me over the years. I played football when I was younger and, for the past 8 years, I've become obsessed with running and trying out various water sports and skiing. However, like many people, during a stressful period in my life I fell into a self-destructive pattern, which included comfort eating and living a sedentary lifestyle. Now that I'm back to exercising regularly, I cannot emphasise enough the value of being active. Apart from the initial benefit of losing weight in my case, regular exercise strengthens the most important muscle of all – the heart. It's also fantastic for relieving stress, something I'm definitely in need of.

A common excuse I know, but finding time to exercise is my biggest problem. My work schedule is very hectic, to say the least. However, exercise needn't always mean running on a treadmill or pumping iron in the gym for hours on end. Quick short walks in the park (or to and from the station or shops) can make a difference. The easiest way to increase your heart rate is to forego the lift or standing on the escalator and climb up the stairs. It works for me whenever I find myself travelling and lacking time for the gym.

As a parent I recognise that it is also important for my children to be active, whether it's playing football, swimming or ballet for the girls. Building good habits from an early age means that they are more likely to participate in physical activity later in life.

Healthy desserts

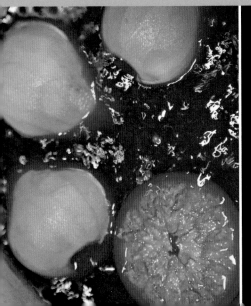

Vanilla pannacotta
with blueberry sauce

blueberries are a great source of antioxidants

Serves 6

600ml whole or semi-skimmed milk

1 vanilla pod, split

125g caster sugar

4 sheets of leaf gelatine

200ml natural yoghurt

Blueberry sauce:

250g blueberries, rinsed and dried

3 tbsp caster sugar or honey

2–3 tbsp lemon juice

Pour the milk into a saucepan and scrape in the seeds from the vanilla pod, adding the pod too. Add the sugar and heat gently, stirring until the sugar has dissolved, then bring to a simmer. Meanwhile, soak the gelatine leaves in cold water for a few minutes to soften them.

As soon as the milk begins to bubble, remove the pan from the heat. Drain the gelatine leaves and squeeze out excess water, then add to the hot milk. Stir to dissolve, then leave to cool before straining through a fine sieve into a bowl.

Add the yoghurt to the infused milk (which must have cooled completely). Pour the mixture into 6 pannacotta or dariole moulds and set them on a tray. Cover with a large piece of cling film and chill for a few hours until set, or overnight.

For the sauce, put the blueberries, sugar and lemon juice into a saucepan. Bring to a simmer and cook for 3 minutes until the berries are soft, but not completely broken down. Transfer to a bowl and leave to cool, then chill.

To unmould each pannacotta, dip the mould in a bowl of warm water for a few seconds, then invert onto a plate and give it a gentle shake to release. If necessary, dilute the blueberry sauce with a tiny splash of water. Spoon a little sauce around each pannacotta and serve.

Pink grapefruit granita with raspberries

fat free and plenty of vitamin C

Put the grapefruit juice, sugar and star anise into a saucepan. Stir over a low heat until the sugar has dissolved, then increase the heat slightly and bring a simmer. Remove from the heat as soon as the juice begins to bubble. Leave to cool completely, then strain and discard the star anise.

Pour the juice into a suitable container and freeze for about 2 hours until it is frozen around the sides and base. Take out of the freezer and use a fork to lightly beat the frozen crystals into the still-liquid centre, then return to the freezer. Repeat beating two or three more times until the granita is frozen with a granular texture.

To serve, scrape the granita with a fork, then spoon into chilled serving glasses. Add a few raspberries to each glass, then pour over a little pink Champagne if you like. Serve at once.

Variations:

- For a refreshing minty flavour, add a handful of mint leaves in place of the star anise.
- For a citrus granita, use equal parts of orange, grapefruit and blood orange juice.
- Spike the granita with 2 tbsp Campari once the juice has cooled down. Serve drizzled with a little Campari instead of Champagne.

Serves 4

500ml pink grapefruit juice, preferably freshly squeezed and strained (3–4 juicy fruit)

75g caster sugar

2 star anise

handful of raspberries

chilled pink Champagne, to serve (optional)

Baked plums
with crushed amaretti

equally delicious with juicy nectarines or peaches

Serves 4

500g ripe, but firm, plums

few small knobs of butter, plus extra to grease

2–3 tbsp crème de cassis or marsala

30g amaretti biscuits

Greek yoghurt, to serve

Heat the oven to 200°C/Gas 6. Cut the plums in half and remove the stones. Arrange the plums halves, cut side up, in a lightly buttered baking dish. Drizzle over the liqueur.

Crush the amaretti biscuits lightly in a large bowl with the end of rolling pin. Sprinkle over the plum halves, then dot a small knob of butter on each fruit. Bake for 10–15 minutes, depending on the ripeness of the plums, until they are soft but still retain their shape. Let cool slightly.

Serve warm, with a dollop of Greek yoghurt.

Spiced apple cake

deliciously dense and moist, with lots of healthy fibre

Serves 8

1kg cooking apples (about 5 or 6)

50g caster sugar

30g butter, plus extra to grease

2 ripe Braeburn or Cox's apples

juice of 1 lemon

225g wholemeal flour

1½ tsp baking powder

½ tsp bicarbonate of soda

¼ tsp fine sea salt

175g soft brown sugar

1 tsp ground cinnamon

1 tsp ground ginger

½ tsp freshly grated nutmeg

½ tsp ground cloves

1 large egg, lightly beaten

50ml light olive oil

2 tbsp apricot jam, to glaze

1–2 tbsp water

Peel, core and slice the cooking apples. Place in a wide pan with the sugar and butter. Cook over a high heat for 10–15 minutes until the apples have broken down to a pulp and any excess water has cooked off. Transfer to a bowl and cool completely. You should have about 475g purée.

Heat the oven to 170°C/Gas 3. Line and lightly grease a 23cm cake tin with a removable base. Peel, core and finely slice the eating apple, using a mandolin or sharp knife. Place in a bowl and pour over most of the lemon juice and a splash of water; set aside.

In a large bowl, mix together the wholemeal flour, baking powder, bicarbonate of soda, salt, sugar and ground spices. Make a well in the centre and add the egg, olive oil and apple purée. Fold into the dry ingredients until just combined.

Transfer the mixture to the prepared cake tin and gently level the top with a spatula. Bake the cake for 30 minutes until it feels just firm to the touch in the centre. Working quickly, overlap the sliced apples in concentric circles on top, leaving a margin around the edge. Brush the slices with a little lemon juice and return to the oven for a further 30–35 minutes until a skewer inserted into the centre comes out clean.

Let the cake cool slightly before unmoulding onto a wire rack. Warm the apricot jam with the water, stirring until smooth. Brush over the top of the cake to glaze. Serve warm.

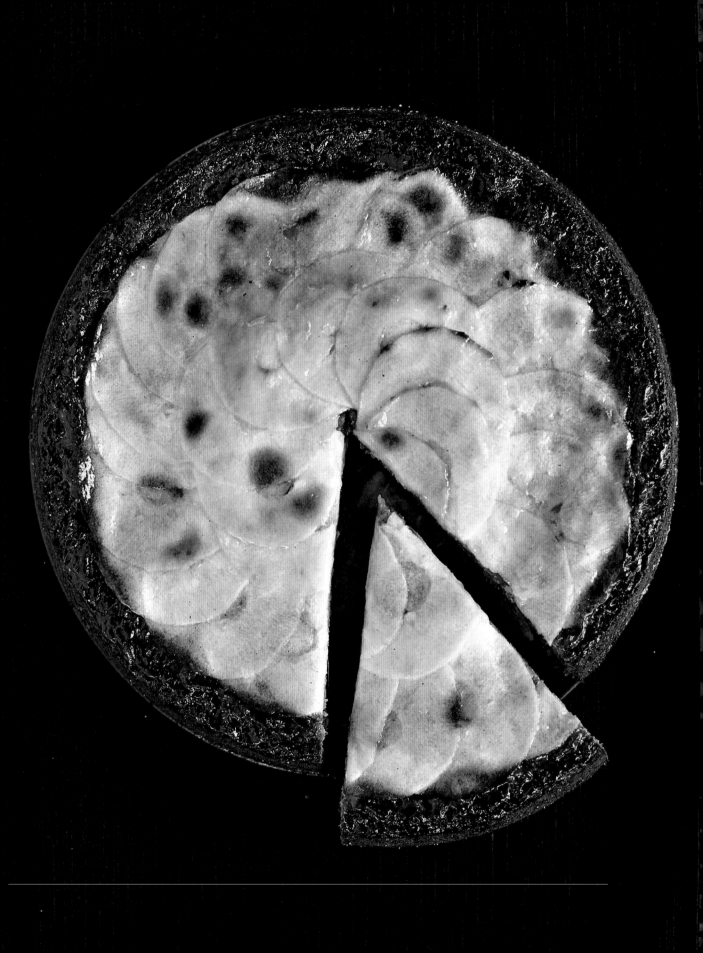

Roasted peaches
with vanilla, spice and honey

use apple juice for an alcohol-free option

Serves 4

4–5 ripe, but firm, peaches

2 cinnamon sticks

2 star anise

1 vanilla pod, split

3–4 tbsp runny honey

generous splash of peach liqueur (or peach schnapps or brandy)

natural or Greek yoghurt, to serve

Heat the oven to 190°C/Gas 5. Cut the peaches in half and prise out the stones. Slice the peach halves into wedges and arrange on a non-stick baking tray. Add the spices and vanilla pod, then drizzle over the honey and peach liqueur.

Bake the peaches for 10–20 minutes until they are just tender and slightly caramelised around the edges. Remove from the oven and leave to cool slightly. Serve with a generous dollop of yoghurt, or spooned over very cold yoghurt sorbet (see page 243).

Pavlova with roasted rhubarb fool

Serves 6

1½ tsp cornflour, plus 1 tsp extra to dust

150g caster sugar

3 large egg whites (ideally from eggs about 1 week old)

1 tsp vanilla extract

½ tsp white wine vinegar

icing sugar, to dust

mint sprigs, to finish

Roasted rhubarb fool:

500g rhubarb, trimmed and roughly chopped

a little butter, to grease

3–4 tbsp caster sugar

a little honey, to drizzle

400ml Greek yoghurt

Heat the oven to 140°C/Gas 1. Draw 6 circles, 8cm in diameter, on a sheet of silicone paper or baking parchment. Invert the paper onto a lightly oiled baking sheet and lightly dust with cornflour. Mix the cornflour with 1 tbsp of the sugar in a small bowl and set aside.

Beat the egg whites in a clean, grease-free bowl to firm peaks, taking care not to overwhisk. Gradually beat in the remaining sugar, 1 tbsp at a time, and whisk until thick and glossy. Fold through the cornflour mixture, vanilla and vinegar.

Spoon the meringue into a large piping bag fitted with a 1–1.5cm plain nozzle. Pipe concentric rounds over each circle to create a disc, then pipe two rings on the rim to form a shell. Bake for 40–45 minutes until dry and crisp. Turn off the oven and leave the meringues to cool slowly inside. (Ideally make them the evening before and leave to cool in the oven overnight.) Peel the meringues off the paper and store in an airtight container.

For the rhubarb, heat the oven to 200°C/Gas 6. Place the rhubarb in a lightly buttered roasting tin, sprinkle with the sugar and toss well. Roast for 15–20 minutes until tender. Tip the rhubarb and juices into a bowl, drizzle with honey and leave to cool completely.

To serve, ripple the roasted rhubarb and juices through the yoghurt to make a fool. Dust the meringue shells with a little icing sugar and place one on each serving plate. Spoon in the rhubarb fool and top with a mint sprig.

5 ways with summerberries

Flavourful, ripe berries are an integral part of my diet in the summer. I swear, there are few better ways to start the day than with an energising smoothie. I simply throw a variety of berries into the blender and whiz them with some low-fat yoghurt and pomegranate or other fruit juice. Packed with vitamins, minerals, antioxidants and fibre, a berry smoothie is a great health boost.

Blueberries are particularly healthy as they have the highest antioxidant capacity. As such, they help to protect the body from cancer and age-related diseases, and promote a healthy skin, eyes and brain. Great to snack on, blueberries can also be added to all kinds of desserts, from fruit salads and fools to crumbles and cheesecakes.

1

Berry crumble

Heat oven to 190°C/Gas 5. For the crumble, put 60g plain flour and 25g chilled diced unsalted butter in a bowl and rub together with your fingertips to a crumbly texture. Stir in 30g demerara sugar and 30g rolled oats. Spread out on a large baking tray and bake for 15 minutes or until golden brown and crisp, giving it a stir halfway through.

Divide 600g mixed berries (blueberries, blackberries, raspberries etc.) between individual ovenproof dishes. Grate a little orange zest over each dish, then halve the orange and squeeze a little juice over the berries. Shred 8 large mint leaves and scatter over the berries along with 1−2 tbsp caster sugar to taste. Top with a layer of crumble. Bake for 10−12 minutes, just to warm through. Serve warm with a dollop of yoghurt. **Serves 4**

2

Mixed berry coulis

Put 150g mixed berries (such as strawberries, raspberries and blueberries) into a blender or food processor with 1 tbsp icing sugar, 2 tbsp lemon juice and 2 tbsp water. Whiz to a purée. If the coulis seems a little too thick, add another 1−2 tbsp water. Pass the mixture through a fine sieve. Use to drizzle over ices, cakes or creamy desserts. **Serves 2−3**

3 Summer berry and vodka jelly

Dissolve 200g caster sugar in 500ml water in a pan over low heat. Meanwhile, soak 3 sheets of leaf gelatine in cold water to soften. Bring the sugar syrup to the boil and let boil for a few minutes. Take off the heat, squeeze the gelatine leaves to remove excess water, then add to the sugar syrup, stirring to dissolve. Leave to cool, then mix in the 60ml vodka.

Mix 200g raspberries, 200g blueberries and 400g hulled and quartered strawberries in a bowl. Shred a handful of basil leaves and toss with the berries, then divide between 5–6 small serving glasses. Pour over just enough of the cooled vodka syrup to cover the berries. Chill for a few hours until set. **Serves 5–6**

4 Raspberry, mango and watercress salad

Peel and thinly slice 1 large ripe mango, avoiding the stone. Trim 200g watercress, removing the stems. Divide the mango and watercress between individual plates and scatter over 75g raspberries. For the dressing, whisk 1 ½ tbsp raspberry vinegar with 4 tbsp extra virgin olive oil, some salt and pepper, and a pinch of caster sugar to taste. Drizzle over the salad and serve, as a starter. **Serves 4**

5 Port and blackberry sauce

Heat 1 tbsp olive oil in a pan and sweat 1 finely chopped large shallot with some seasoning for 4–6 minutes until soft. Pour in 75ml port and let bubble until reduced by two-thirds. Add 150g blackberries, 150ml chicken stock (see page 249) and 2 tbsp redcurrant jelly. Bring to a simmer and cook for 8–10 minutes until thickened to the desired consistency. Strain and serve as an accompaniment to duck, game and pork. **Serves 4**

Poached pears
in mulled wine

easy prepare-ahead dessert

Serves 4

750ml bottle of red wine

4 tbsp caster sugar

2 cinnamon sticks

½ tsp cloves

2 orange slices

1 stem ginger in syrup, halved

4 ripe, but firm, pears, such as Williams

Pour the red wine into a medium saucepan and add the sugar, spices, orange slices and stem ginger. Slowly bring to a simmer, stirring initially to dissolve the sugar. Simmer gently for 15–20 minutes to allow the aromatics to infuse their flavours into the wine.

Peel each pear, leaving the stalk on, and scoop out the core from the base with a melon baller. Gently lower the pears into the mulled wine. Rest a crumpled piece of greaseproof paper with a small hole cut out in the centre on top; this will help to keep the pears submerged in the liquid.

Poach the pears for 10–20 minutes, depending on ripeness. To test, pierce with a fine metal skewer – it should meet with little resistance. Transfer the pears and mulled wine to a large bowl and leave to cool. Cover with cling film and refrigerate overnight to allow the flavours to develop.

Serve the pears warm, reheating them gently, or at room temperature, with a scoop of vanilla ice cream or yoghurt sorbet (see page 243) if you like.

Camomile and ginger jelly
with ginger melon

Serves 4–6

10g camomile tea or 2 camomile teabags

85g caster sugar

finger length knob of fresh root ginger, thickly sliced

500ml boiling water

3 sheets of leaf gelatine

Ginger melon:

75g granulated or caster sugar

75ml water

small knob of fresh root ginger, peeled and cut into matchsticks

1 Charentais or a small honeydew melon

Put the camomile tea, sugar and ginger into a warmed large teapot. Pour in the boiling water, put the lid on and leave to infuse for 4–5 minutes. Meanwhile, soak the gelatine leaves in cold water to cover for a few minutes to soften.

Strain the infused tea into a jug and discard the tea and ginger pieces. Drain and squeeze out the excess water from the gelatine leaves, then add to the hot tea and stir to dissolve. Leave to cool completely. Pour into individual serving glasses and chill for 6 hours or longer until the jellies have set.

For the ginger melon, dissolve the sugar in the water in a small pan over a low heat, stirring occasionally. Increase the heat and bring to the boil, then add the ginger and simmer for 5 minutes. Remove from the heat and set aside to infuse until cold.

Cut the melon in half and remove the seeds. Scoop out the flesh into balls, using a melon baller, and place in a large bowl. Strain the infused syrup over the melon. Leave to macerate for 10 minutes.

To serve, spoon a few melon balls onto each jelly and drizzle with a little of the syrup.

Lime mousse

Serves 8

2 sheets of leaf gelatine

juice of 4 limes (about 150ml)

175g caster sugar

2 medium egg whites

200ml reduced-fat crème fraîche

1–2 limes, for zesting

Soak the gelatine leaves in cold water to cover for a few minutes to soften. Meanwhile, put the lime juice in a measuring jug and top up with cold water to reach 200ml. Pour into a saucepan and add half the sugar. Stir over a low heat to dissolve, then increase the heat and bring to a simmer. Take the pan off the heat.

Drain the gelatine leaves and squeeze out excess water, then add to the lime syrup and stir to dissolve. Leave to cool completely.

Beat the egg whites in a clean, grease-free bowl with an electric whisk until they form stiff peaks. Beat in the remaining sugar, 1 tbsp at a time, until fully incorporated and the meringue is firm.

In another bowl, lightly beat the crème fraîche, then stir in the cooled lime mixture. (The mixture will be quite loose and thin at this stage.) Fold through the meringue, then spoon the mixture into small serving glasses.

Chill the mousses for a few hours to firm up a little. Grate over a little lime zest to finish before serving.

tangy, soft set mousse, rich in vitamin C

Ricotta cheesecake
with orange and cinnamon

low-fat baked cheesecake

Serves 8

Crust:

40g lightly salted butter, melted, plus extra to grease

150g reduced-fat digestive biscuits

1 medium egg white, lightly beaten

Ricotta filling:

500g ricotta cheese

250g quark

100g caster sugar

1 tbsp cornflour

3 large eggs

finely grated zest of 1 orange

2–3 tbsp Grand Marnier or Cointreau, to taste

½ tsp ground cinnamon

Oranges in syrup (optional):

4 large navel oranges

50g caster sugar

60ml Grand Marnier or Cointreau

Heat the oven to 150°C/Gas 2. Lightly butter a deep 20cm cake tin with a removable base.

For the crust, break up the biscuits and whiz in a food processor to fine crumbs. Add the melted butter and pulse until the mixture comes together. Tip into the prepared tin and press down firmly with the back of a spoon to create a neat crust. Stand the tin on a baking sheet and bake for 10–12 minutes until lightly browned. As you remove it from the oven, brush the crust with the egg white. Leave to cool slightly. Clean the processor.

For the ricotta filling, whiz all the ingredients in the food processor until well blended. You may need to stop the machine to scrape down the sides once or twice. Pour the filling over the crust and bake for 30 minutes until it has just set around the sides but is still quite runny in the middle.

Turn off the heat but leave the cheesecake in the oven to cool slowly; the filling will continue to set as it cools. Leave until completely cooled, preferably overnight.

To prepare the oranges if serving, cut away the peel and pith, then slice into rounds and place in a bowl. Heat a heavy-based frying pan until hot, add the sugar and let it caramelise over a high heat. Protecting your hand (as the mixture will splutter), add the liqueur and a small splash of water. The caramel may harden, but it will soften and return to a syrup as you stir over a low heat. Pour over the orange slices and toss to coat.

To serve, run a knife around the cheesecake and unmould onto a plate. Serve with the oranges in syrup if desired.

Yoghurt sorbet

a refreshing low-fat alternative to ice cream

Pour the water into a heavy-based pan, add the sugar and liquid glucose and place over a low heat. Stir occasionally until the sugar has dissolved, then increase the heat and boil for 3–4 minutes. Remove from the heat and cool completely.

Beat the yoghurt and fromage frais together in a bowl until smooth and creamy. Mix in the cooled syrup.

Pour the mixture into an ice-cream machine and churn until almost firm, then scoop the sorbet into a suitable container and freeze for several hours until firm. If you do not have an ice-cream machine, freeze the mixture in a shallow container and beat with a fork several times during freezing.

Delicious served with both hot and cold desserts, or scooped into glasses with fresh fruit.

Variations:

- Purée ½ ripe but firm mango and chop the other half. Fold the purée into the sorbet mixture before freezing; fold in the chopped mango halfway through churning.
- Purée the flesh of 2–3 ripe skinned nectarines or peaches until smooth and fold into the sorbet base before freezing.
- Reduce the water to 300ml. Add the finely grated zest and juice of 2 limes to the sorbet mixture before freezing. Serve with griddled pineapple wedges.

Serves 6–8

350ml water

225g caster sugar

3 tbsp liquid glucose

300ml natural yoghurt

100ml fromage frais

Chocolate mousse

a lighter version of my cook-along recipe

150g dark chocolate, in pieces, plus an extra 25g for grating

2 chocolate-coated honeycomb bars (Crunchie bars)

100g caster sugar

1 tsp liquid glucose

2 tbsp water

2 large egg whites

100ml crème fraîche

1–2 tbsp Kahlua or other coffee liqueur (optional)

Melt the chocolate in a heatproof bowl set over a pan of simmering water. Meanwhile, put the honeycomb bars into the freezer for 10 minutes. When the chocolate has melted, remove from the heat and set aside.

For the meringue, put the sugar, liquid glucose and water into a saucepan and place over a low heat until the sugar has dissolved, stirring a couple of times. Increase the heat and boil the syrup until it registers 120°C on a sugar thermometer; ie the 'hard ball stage', when a little of the hot syrup dropped into a glass of water hardens to a form a clear ball.

Meanwhile, beat the egg whites in a clean, grease-free bowl to stiff peaks. With the beaters working, slowly trickle the hot syrup onto the egg whites. Continue to whisk until the egg whites are smooth, glossy and have tripled in volume. The sides of the bowl should no longer feel hot.

Add the crème fraîche to the melted chocolate and whisk to combine. Fold the chocolate mixture into the meringue, followed by the coffee liqueur if using.

Remove the wrapper from one of the chilled honeycomb bars and wrap in a clean tea-towel. Place on a board and bash lightly with a rolling pin to crush the honeycomb. Open up the tea-towel and tip the crushed honeycomb into the mousse, then gently fold through with a spatula.

Spoon the mousse into small serving dishes set on a tray. Grate over a layer of chocolate-coated honeycomb, followed by a layer of chocolate. Chill for a few hours before serving.

Healthy basics

Vegetable stock

Makes about 1.5 litres

3 onions, peeled and roughly chopped

1 leek, washed and roughly chopped

2 celery sticks, roughly chopped

6 carrots, peeled and roughly chopped

1 head of garlic, halved crossways

1 tsp white peppercorns

1 bay leaf

few thyme, basil, tarragon, coriander and parsley sprigs, tied together

200ml dry white wine

sea salt and black pepper

Put the vegetables, garlic, peppercorns and bay leaf in a large stockpot and pour on cold water to cover, about 2 litres. Bring to the boil, lower the heat to a simmer and leave to cook gently for 20 minutes. Remove the pan from the heat and add the bundle of herbs, white wine and a little seasoning. Give the stock a stir and leave to cool completely.

Chill the stock overnight before straining if you have time. Pass through a fine sieve into a bowl. Refrigerate and use within 5 days, or freeze in smaller amounts for up to 3 months.

Fish stock

Makes about 1 litre

2 tbsp olive oil

1 small onion, peeled and chopped

½ celery stick, sliced

1 small fennel bulb, chopped

sea salt and black pepper

1kg white fish bones and trimmings (or crab or lobster shells)

75ml dry white wine

Heat the olive oil in a stockpot and add the onion, celery, fennel and a little seasoning. Stir over a medium heat for 3–4 minutes until the vegetables begin to soften but not brown. Add the fish bones and trimmings and the wine, then pour in enough cold water to cover the ingredients. Simmer for 20 minutes, then remove the pan from the heat and leave to cool.

Ladle the stock through a fine sieve into a bowl and discard the solids. Refrigerate and use within 2 days, or freeze in smaller quantities for up to 3 months.

Chicken stock

Makes about 1.5 litres

2 tbsp olive oil

1 carrot, peeled and chopped

1 onion, peeled and chopped

2 celery sticks, chopped

1 leek, washed and sliced

1 bay leaf

1 thyme sprig

3 garlic cloves, peeled

2 tbsp tomato purée

2 tbsp plain flour

1kg raw chicken bones

sea salt and black pepper

Heat the olive oil in a large stockpot and add the vegetables, herbs and garlic. Cook over a medium heat, stirring occasionally, until the vegetables are golden. Stir in the tomato purée and flour and cook for another minute. Add the chicken bones, then pour in enough cold water to cover. Season lightly. Bring to the boil and skim off any scum that rises to the surface. Reduce the heat and leave to simmer gently for 1 hour.

Let the stock stand for a few minutes, then pass through a fine sieve and leave to cool. Refrigerate and use within 5 days, or freeze the stock in convenient portions for up to 3 months.

Beef stock

Makes about 1.5 litres

1.5 kg beef or veal marrow bones, chopped into 5–6cm pieces

2 tbsp olive oil, plus extra to drizzle

2 onions, peeled

2 carrots, peeled

2 celery stalks, peeled

1 large fennel bulb, trimmed

1 tbsp tomato purée

100g button mushrooms

1 bay leaf

1 thyme sprig

1 tsp black peppercorns

Heat the oven to 220°C/Gas 7. Put the bones in a roasting tray and drizzle with a little olive oil. Roast for about 1 hour, turning over halfway, until evenly browned. Meanwhile, cut the onions, carrots, celery and fennel into 5cm chunks.

Heat the olive oil in a large stockpot and add the vegetables. Cook, stirring frequently, over a high heat until golden brown. Stir in the tomato purée and cook for another 2 minutes. Add the browned bones and pour in enough water (about 2–2.5 litres) to cover them and the vegetables. Bring to a simmer and skim off the froth and scum that rise to the surface. Add the mushrooms, bay leaf, thyme and peppercorns. Simmer for 6–8 hours until the stock has a deep, rich flavour.

Leave to stand for a few minutes, then pass the stock through a fine sieve. Leave to cool, then refrigerate and use within 5 days, or freeze in smaller portions for up to 3 months.

INDEX

Acknowledgements

Once more, I am indebted to my marvelous team who time and again astound me with their creativity and commitment. They were pushed to the limits and worked incredibly hard to put this fantastic book together at breakneck speed. Specifically, my special thanks to Mark Sargeant who has worked with me for a long time and plays such a vital role; Emily Quah for brilliantly ensuring that the recipes in the book are mouth-wateringly delicious and healthy; Helen Lewis for making the book look so smart and beautiful; Lisa Barber for her great photography; Janet Illsley for her amazing editorial thoroughness; Nicola for her intensive work on the layouts; and Anne Furniss and Alison Cathie at Quadrille for their continual support.

Also to Pat Llewellyn and her team at Optomen for producing a fantastic new series; Chris Hutcheson and everyone at Gordon Ramsay Holdings who keep the business running smoothly while we focus on producing great food, books and television; and finally to my talented wife, Tana, and our mums, Helen and Greta, for helping to care for the zoo while we work.

Project director Anne Furniss
Creative director Helen Lewis
Project editor Janet Illsley
Photographer Lisa Barber
Food stylist Mark Sargeant
Home economist Emily Quah, assisted by Cathryn Evans
Design assistant Nicola Davidson
Production Vincent Smith, Ruth Deary

Optomen Television:
Managing director Pat Llewellyn
F Word executive producers Jon Swain and Ben Adler
Series producer Sarah Lazenby
Food producer Sarah Durdin Robertson

Optomen Television Limited
1, Valentine Place
London SE1 8QH
www.optomen.com

First published in 2008 by
Quadrille Publishing Limited
Alhambra House, 27-31 Charing Cross Road,
London WC2H 0LS
www.quadrille.co.uk

Text © 2008 Gordon Ramsay
Photography © 2008 ▮▮▮▮▮▮ Quadrille Publishing Limited
Design and layout © 2008 Quadrille Publishing Limited
Format and programme © 2008 Optomen Television Limited

Cataloguing in Publication Data: a catalogue record for this book is available from the British Library.

ISBN 978 184400 636 6

Printed in Italy